INDIO

Reflections and Visions

Commemorating Seventy-Five Years
1930 - 2005

Victoria J. Bailey
DESERT SPRINGS PUBLISHING
2005

Mt. San Jacinto, near Indio, on
the Sunset Route of the Southern
Pacific Railroad.

Out Where The West Begins

Out where the West begins
Out where the handclasp's a little stronger,
Out where the smile dwells a little longer,
That's where the West begins;
Out where the sun is a little brighter,
Where the snows that fall are a trifle whiter,
Where the bonds of home are a wee bit tighter,
That's where the West begins.

Out where the skies are a trifle bluer,
Out where friendship's a little truer,
That's where the West begins;
Where there's laughter in every streamlet flowing,
Where there's more of reaping and less of sowing,
That's where the West begins.

Out where the world is in the making,
Where fewer hearts with despair are aching,
That's where the West begins;
Where there's more of singing and less of sighing,
Where there's more of giving and less of buying,
And a man makes friends without half trying,
That's where the West begins.

POEM FROM THE EARLY WEST

Reprinted from antique postcard, circa 1930, author unknown.

DESERT SPRINGS PUBLISHING

Victoria J. Bailey, *Publisher and Founder*
Michael G. Morein, *Associate Publisher*
Gayl Biondi, *Editorial Director*
Becky Kurtz, *Editor*
Sharon O'Donnell, *Contributing Researcher*
Karen Oppenheim, *Contributing Profile Writer*

CONTRIBUTING PHOTOGRAPHY

Bruce Clark, Paul Ames, Cherry Ishimatsu, Ben Guitron, Sharon O'Donnell,
Jens Harboe, Dave Henderson, Esther Acosta, Linda Beal

CONTRIBUTING PHOTOGRAPHS

Coachella Valley Museum and Cultural Center, Riverside County Fire Department,
Coachella Valley Water District, Indio Chamber of Commerce, City of Indio,
Indio Senior Center, Kiki Haynes Photography, Cabazon Museum, Riverside County Fair and
National Date Festival, JFK Memorial Hospital, Dr. Carreon Foundation

ART DIRECTION, DESIGN AND PRODUCTION

Eaton & Kirk Advertising
John Kirkpatrick, *Creative Director*
Ramsey Lucas, *Graphic Designer*

COVER DESIGN

Eaton & Kirk Advertising
John Kirkpatrick, *Creative Director*

Desert Springs Publishing
78-365 Highway 111, Suite 340, La Quinta, CA 92253
760-219-7008
Email: victoria@desertspringspublishing.com
www.desertspringspublishing.com
www.californiadesertresortcities.com

Eaton & Kirk Advertising
47-159 Youngs Lane, Indio, CA 92201
760-775-3626
info@EatonKirk.com
www.EatonKirk.com

ISBN 0-9727572-3-6 First Edition

Copyright 2005 by Desert Springs Publishing

Published 2005
Toppan Printing Company of (HK) Ltd.
Printed in China

Table of Contents

Acknowledgments

Within the framework of all the many wonderful celebrations that mark the City of Indio's 75th anniversary, it is my heartfelt belief that *Indio Reflections and Visions* will merit a lasting impact.

For now we can enjoy traveling back in time and learning about, and in some cases reliving, our rich heritage. Now there is a fresh compilation of what came before coupled with a chronicle of our boundless enthusiasm for the future that we can share with generations to come.

Indio Reflections and Visions could not have been a reality without the vision of Ken Weller, interim city manager, who realized the importance of telling the City's story. He had heard that, as a relative newcomer to the Coachella Valley, I was so enamored with my new community that I launched Desert Springs Publishing Company and published *California Desert Resort Cities Reflections & Visions*, a year after arriving here from the Bay Area.

My first major hardcover book, *San Francisco Gold Rush to Cyberspace*, celebrated that City's and Chamber's 150th anniversary.

But no one can do it alone. Thanks to the many businesses that supported this effort through participation in the Profiles of Excellence. And to the enthusiastic assistance of staffs at the Indio Chamber of Commerce and the City of Indio — with a most special thanks to Mark Wasserman, administrative project manager. Together, along with many of our community's dedicated ambassadors, we have created "a loving tribute."

Special thanks to the Coachella Valley Historical Society, Museum & Cultural Center and to the Indio Senior Center for their generous sharing of information and photographs.

Indio Reflections and Visions has truly been a labor of love.

—Victoria J. Bailey, Publisher

Forward

A SPECIAL INTRODUCTION BY WILLIAM DEVANE

Indio typifies the true spirit of the West. Indio's settlers weathered the test of time by taming the land and making it their own. Imagine how difficult it must have been in those early days in this once remote desert outpost. Now look around today at the thriving community Indio has become and marvel at the accomplishments of the Indio spirit.

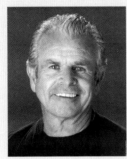

WILLIAM DEVANE

I'm a proud owner of a successful business, Devane's Restaurant, in Indio. I might be considered a "newcomer," so I enjoy meeting the people of Indio and hearing their fascinating stories about the history and growth of Indio.

A fine example of Indio's strength of character was Olaf J. "Ole" Nordland who came to Indio in 1948 as editor of the Indio Daily News *and served as archivist of the Coachella Valley Historical Society until his death in 1985. One of the best descriptions of the opportunities and sacrifices that made Indio what it is today exists in Ole Nordland's 1976 editorial marking the 100th anniversary of the arrival of the railroad in Indio.*

This book salutes courage like Ole's and the heart and soul of all those who came before us to build Indio for us to love and enjoy.

—William Devane

How Much Did It Cost To Get Where We Are?

It has been said we cannot know how far we can go until we know how far we have come. We ought to know how much it cost to get where we are today. There is no doubt but that the 1876 arrival and building of the Southern Pacific Railroad through this valley was the first important event in our centennial history.

Ole Nordland

The railroad made another contribution in discovering the great reservoir of artesian water underlying this area which led to irrigation of this portion of the Colorado Desert. The two events led to many of the great things that have happened to us since.

A common theme of the earliest settlers was that "we should have pride in our heritage, but it's here that you live. This is the land that will have to yield its bread." Every man was out to make his mark and didn't expect any special dispensation from his government to assure his success or opportunity.

During my personal search and collection of history of this area, I have been impressed by the vigor and spirit of the early settlers in what was pretty much a hostile environment. Always remember that if the past can tell us something about our potential as a people, about the worth of our ideals and about courage and strength and vision (which are our heritage), we all need to know about it with pride.

—Editorial by Ole Nordland, published in the INDIO DAILY NEWS *on May 29, 1976*

Indio Then and Now

**CITY FACTS
AT A GLANCE
1930 / 2005**

POPULATION
1,875 (1930)
59,133 (2005)

AREA
.31 square miles (1930)
24.8 square miles (2005)

CITY BUDGET
$4,791 (1930)
$34,931,649 (2005)

**ASSESSED
VALUATION**
$479,160 (1930)
$418,685,078 (2005)

*Incorporated on Friday,
May 16, 1930.*

*The first Indio City Hall
was located at the corner
of Smurr Street and
Highway 99.*

EDUCATION

Above: First Indio school located on the N.E. corner of Fargo and Bliss, circa 1900.
Right: Jackson Community School after extensive remodel, 2004.

HOUSING

Above: This tent house was typical of most "first homes" in 1907.
Right: This home at Indian Springs Golf and Country Club is one of the many lifestyles available in Indio, 2005.

75 Years of Progress

TRANSPORTATION

Above: A paved highway from Edom to Indio cost $104,840, circa 1930.
Right: Indio Boulevard Enhancement Project, Ground Breaking Ceremony, January 2004. Left to right, Assistant City Manager Ken Weller, City Council Member Ben Godfrey, City Council Member Melanie Fesmire, City Council Member Mike Wilson and City Manager Tom Ramirez.

PUBLIC SAFETY

Above: Early fire truck, circa 1900.
Right: Indio Fire Department, left to right, Fire Captain Dave LaClair, FF/Paramedic Brian Flint, Fire Captain Mike Smith, Firefighter Ignatio Otero, Firefighter Matt Misenhimer, Firefighter Travis Ames, FF/Paramedic Scott Dryden, FF/Paramedic Kyle Smith, Firefighter Ricardo Ginese and Battalion Chief Tom Hyatt.

INDIO, CALIFORNIA

Towne Street and Smurr Street were named after Southern Pacific officials.

Miles Avenue was named for General Miles, who became famous in the Indian War and visited Indio in 1903. He is said to have spoken graciously to the town's schoolchildren. Locals were so grateful and impressed they named a street in his honor.

Professor William P. Blake and a U.S. Army survey party are credited with establishing an east-west wagon route through the San Gorgonio Pass in the late 1800s, closely resembling what is now Varner Road north of Interstate 10.

Indio Becomes A City

Indio's incorporation came on the heels of the Great Depression and marked a turning point for America's western expansion. In the 75 years since, Indio has built on its civic pride while world events shaped our modern day society.

In 1930, Herbert Hoover was President and money was scarce. People did what they could to amuse themselves. Movies were all the rage, while board games and parlor games were popular. Communities celebrated with local parades and fun sport activities.

1929 - Greyhound Bus Lines promotes service to Indio

1930 - Indio becomes the Coachella Valley's first incorporated city

1934 - Al Capone's train passes through Indio on its way to Alcatraz

1936 - The founder of Bank of America visits Indio declaring the Depression over and citing Indio as a "Community of the Future"

1949 - Hotel Indio guests enjoy the luxury of a new technology - evaporative coolers

1953 - Aviatrix Jackie Cochran sets three world records testing jet aircraft at Edwards Air Force Base

1959 - *The Date Palm* newspaper becomes *The Indio News*

1966 - The historic Southern Pacific Depot in Indio is destroyed by fire

1973 - United Farm Workers labor union organizers disrupt valley agriculture

1984 - Coachella Valley Museum opens

2000 - 1st Coachella Music & Arts Festival at Empire Polo Grounds

Indio Civic Club during Western Days. From left to right, Wallace P. Rouse, A. Rolland, F. A. Purcell, F. G. Tebo, C. A. Washburn, and Hugh Moore.

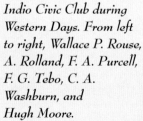

Indio's incorporation was a hard-fought battle. The first City Council faced a host of challenges. In 1971, then Indio Daily News reporter, Jeri Taylor, studied the archives of the early City Council minutes to chronicle the start of Indio's civic structure.

Founding Fathers Faced Host Of Decisions

By Jeri Taylor
DAILY NEWS STAFF WRITER
September 23, 1971

The first meeting of the Indio City Council was June 4, 1930. The first item on the agenda was the appointment of a city manager. Somehow the action got lost in the shuffle, because the city did not hire its first city manager, R. C. O'Reilly, until 1953.

At the second meeting, two weeks later, the council approved the purchase of $430 worth of blank paper and forms that they believed would be a year's supply. After the purchase was approved, the group realized it had no money with which to operate. Mayor Leroy Pawley withdrew a dollar bill from his wallet and presented it to the city clerk "to show that the City of Indio is not without funds."

By the third meeting, the subject of business licenses was brought up as a source of revenue. After the required number of readings, the Business License Ordinance, Number 5 in the city ledger, became law. The largest fee was pronounced on laundries, the smallest on shoemakers. The average business fee for merchants and professional men was $7.50 per quarter.

Near the beginning of September, Francis A. Koehler was appointed as the first Chief of Police. His salary was set at $75 per month. Later the city's first policeman was hired, and his stipend was $125 per month - the unusual difference was never commented upon.

Disenchantment with the new government caused citizens to bring a petition to the October 16 meeting to nullify the incorporation. The city attorney determined that 19 of the petition names were illegal, another 25 chose to withdraw, and the subject was ultimately dropped.

At the November 21 meeting, parking time limits were enacted for downtown due to the heavy traffic. At the January 5, 1931 meeting, the merchants on Fargo Street appeared to protest the state's use of Fargo Street for the testing of automobile headlights. They said the testing always took place on Saturday and was ruining business.

INDIO NOW

Seventy-Five Years of

Amelia Earhart and Jackie Cochran share a moment beside the pool at the Cochran-Odlum ranch in Indio, circa 1936.

Left to right, Johnny Dawson, Helen Dettweiler, Jackie Cochran and Randolf Scott.

Indio Mayors: 1930-1980

1930 - 32	Leroy A. Pawley
1932 - 34	Edward W. Johnston
1934 - 36	Walter S. Dodge
1936 - 41	Harry Moore
1940 - 41	Byron Peebler
1941 - 46	Clarence Washburn
1946 - 48	John Neal Filer
1948 - 52	Clarence Washburn
1952 - 54	Peter A. Jannotta
1954 - 56	Gordon Cologne
1956 - 58	Clarence Washburn
1958 - 60	B. W. Burkhardt
1960 - 62	James J. O'Brien
1962 - 65	Franklin R. Thompson
1965 - 66	Joseph C. Patterson
1966 - 68	Max T. McCandless
1968 - 70	T. W. Overhulse, D.V.M.
1970 - 72	Joseph C. Patterson
1972 - 74	Roger M. Harlow
1974 - 79	Raymond M. Rinderhagen
1979 - 80	Regena M. Zokosky

Jack Dempsey and Joe DeCoster, circa 1960.

Leaders & Luminaries

Former President Dwight D. Eisenhower and guest. At left, former President John F. Kennedy.

Signing of the Salton Sea Advisory Committee Bill on June 27, 1968 was commemorated in this photo which includes Governor Ronald Regan, Senator Ralph Dills and Senator Gordon Cologne, who represented the Coachella Valley in Sacramento.

Indio Mayors: 1980-2006

1980 - 81	Phillip A. Reed
	David Hernandez
1981 - 84	Roger M. Harlow
1984 - 85	John E. Burrow
1985 - 89	Darwin D. Oakley
1989 - 91	James FitzHenry
1991 - 92	Marcos Lopez
1992 - 93	Jeffrey Holt
1993 - 94	Elfrieda L. Hall
1994 - 95	Tom Hunt
1995 - 96	Marcos Lopez
1996 - 97	Jeffrey Holt
1997	Charles J. Cervello
	Michael H. Wilson
1998 - 99	Chris Silva
1999 - 00	Marcos Lopez
2000 - 01	Melanie Fesmire
2001 - 02	Ben Godfrey
2002 - 03	Michael H. Wilson
2003 - 04	Jacqueline Bethel
2004 - 06	Melanie Fesmire

Land of Plenty

*Historic Mural: Desert Cahuilla Village,
corner of Indio Boulevard and Towne Street,
artist Don Gray, completed 1999.*

*Sunset Route, Southern
Pacific Railroad,
Los Angeles through
Indio to Arizona.*

Land of Plenty

By the time modern explorers came upon what is now Indio, native people had made this part of the great Southwest their home for thousands of years. The ancestors of our local Indian tribes are estimated to have ventured into the Coachella Valley from the Colorado River over 900 years ago.

They built villages near hot springs, migrating to cooler mountain villages during summer. At the time, ancient Lake Cahuilla covered 2,000 square miles of the Imperial and Coachella valleys, extending from present day Indio to below the Mexican border. The Indians hunted wild game and gathered bountiful plant-based foods in a region of diverse landscapes and climates, from the arid desert floor to the pine-topped mountains.

Beginning in the late 1700s, Spanish and Mexican explorers spread the word about the paradise they found while searching for a supply route from Mexico to the Catholic missions throughout California. When early pioneers came to the Coachella Valley, they found the Cahuilla Indians well established with two groups of clans - the Wildcat and Coyote, each with numerous smaller clans using their own name, territory and common ancestry.

In 1849, the Gold Rush lured prospectors from all over the world to stake their claims in the Wild West. The following year, California became a state. By the 1850s, the Cahuilla Indian population in the Indio area began to dwindle. When President Ulysses S. Grant issued an executive order on May 15, 1876, creating the Cabazon Reservation, there were 600 tribal members. Today, there are less than 50 members of the Cabazon Band of Mission Indians.

THE CAHUILLA INDIANS

The word "Indio" is Spanish for Indian.

Cahuilla (pronounced Kah-we-ah) means "master" or "powerful one."

A family residence, a dome made of reeds, branches and brush, was known as a kish.

It is believed the Cahuilla are the only American natives who dug wells to tap underground water for a stable water supply system.

Chief Cabazon was the leader of the Desert Cahuilla Indians for most of the 1800s.

THE RAILROAD

1847 - *Jefferson Davis proposes a southern transcontinental railroad*
1865 - *Southern Pacific Railroad is founded*
1869 - *The last spike is driven to complete the first transcontinental line*
1878 - *The Indio depot and hotel is completed*
1895 - *Albert Tingman gets permission to name the townsite Indio*
1910 - *Southern Pacific introduces dining cars on trains*
1925 - *U.S. Route 99 opens, providing another way to travel to Indio*
1950 - *Travel by bus further undermines rail travel*
1966 - *An early morning fire destroys the Indio depot and hotel*

Southern Pacific engine 3033, at right, was the fastest passenger train and rated at 83 miles per hour.

The Southern Pacific Railroad

The pace of American society was picking up rapidly. The Southern Pacific Railroad laid claim to local water rights. Railroad tycoons raced to build a transcontinental line to transport goods (and the settlers to buy them) from the East Coast to the West. As the halfway point between Los Angeles and Yuma, Arizona, Indio was chosen as the Southern Pacific's desert headquarters. Local train service started in the spring of 1876 with three trips to Los Angeles per week on a train called the Sidewinder.

> *Much of the food served to transcontinental travelers came from local residents. Otho Moore sold watermelons to the depot for one dollar each. The depot would, in turn, sell watermelon to customers for fifty cents a slice.*
> **Excerpt from**
> ***Indio: Southern Pacific Railroad Town***
> **by Jean-Guy Tanner Dube**

The depot became the focal point and social center of the community. The building itself was innovative in its architectural design and its engineering. Experimental gardens showed off the bounty that could be grown with reclaimed desert land. The steel rails brought those in poor health looking for a healing climate as well as eager homesteaders looking for opportunities on the new frontier.

The depot/hotel provided jobs for cooks, waiters and clerks. "The club is feeding 800 people per day and does a total business of $8,000 per month. The terminal's business has grown into the most important feeding station on the entire Southern Pacific system," reported the *Indio Date Palm* newspaper.

Joe DeCoster, who lived in Indio until his death in 2004, was an engineer with Southern Pacific from 1934 to 1985. He remembered renting a bed on the 2nd floor of the Indio Depot/Hotel for 25 cents per night and working on the Yellow Belly line by day. Joe said he loved working on the railroad because "the scenes were always different."

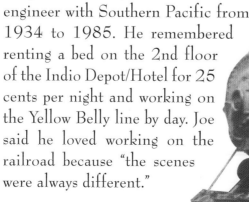

Southern Pacific built a pipeline north of Palm Springs to catch water coming down from the mountains at Snow Creek to feed their thirsty steam locomotives. Some of the precious water that was hauled in was diverted to irrigate fields where crops were grown to feed railroad workers and train passengers. Much like looking for a needle in a haystack, the railroad drilled in the desert for many years without success for a useable source of water.

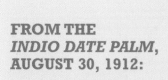

Railroad officials were undaunted by the scarcity of water in the desert. Since they were making a considerable investment in Indio as a rail center, they figured the quickest way to find water was to create a need for it. No slouches at clever marketing, Southern Pacific sent boxcars outfitted with ice and packed full of Coachella Valley produce and citrus back to the Midwest. They advertised that anyone who bought farmland in the Coachella Valley would receive free return passage.

Gertrude Reusch Jones, employed by the Southern Pacific Railroad, was a resident of Indio for nearly 30 years. She came to the valley with her husband in October, 1911. They resided on Bliss Avenue until she passed away in July, 1938.

Above: Pictured here are Marqueritta and Frances Ford, children of Mr. and Mrs. Ford, Southern Pacific Depot Hotel Dining Room managers, circa 1905.

"From this valley of Indio there are to come oranges equaling in lusciousness and flavor those of Hermosillo; tobacco excelling that of Vuelto Aajo of Cuba for cigars; and grapes the size and flavor to produce wines superior to Johannisberger. The succulent watermelon grows to supernatural size. Its climate is absolutely perfection; ten months in the year is paradise; a perfect sanitarium for invalids with throat and lung difficulties."
—**L.F. Scott, Southern Pacific Land Agent, 1892**

"For many years I have seen indisputable evidence of the benefit derived from the climate of Indio. Persons suffering from rheumatism, asthma, and nervous prostration are all benefited. The aridity soothes and rests, and thus benefits those who have been suffering from a nervous strain. The physician who has a patient suffering from insomnia can conscientiously send him to Indio."
—**Dr. Walter Lindley, University of Southern California, 1888**

Artesian well located at the Cawthon Ranch.

Above right, well drilled by Martin & Sanford on the Thayer Brothers Ranch at Avenue 61 and Pierce in 1910. Left to right, Royal B. Thayer and well driller Grant Thompson. At far right, A. B. (Bud) Martin. Beside him is Fred Thayer.

Water Makes Its Mark

Anxious to populate the new western frontier, the U.S. government surveyed sections of land 10 miles square along both sides of the railroad tracks. They numbered the parcels and assigned the odd numbered ones to the railroad. Eventually, the even-numbered sections were awarded to the Cahuilla Indians, creating a "checkerboard" development pattern across the valley.

When well diggers for the railroad finally hit a gusher after almost 20 years, it proved not only to be plentiful but pure. They had stumbled into one of the largest underground aquifers in the state, extending the length of the Coachella Valley. Water flowing down the snow-capped mountain ranges surrounding the valley was already of high quality. Once it percolated through hundreds of feet of sand, it flowed into a giant subterranean lake, or aquifer. Hydrologists later confirmed that the water was exceptionally pure.

The Coachella Valley is part of a natural geologic depression, the bottom of which reaches 265 feet below sea level. With the soft underground strata kept under pressure by a hard surface of rock, conditions were perfect for artesian wells. By 1900, there were six different well drilling enterprises in the Coachella Valley. By 1908, more than 500 wells had been drilled.

Not long after geologists confirmed the existence of artesian wells, and well diggers were busy tapping into the underground resource, townspeople began to worry about laying claim to supplemental water. Southern Pacific was busy taking farming to the next level by encouraging the establishment of a distribution system for year-round produce. They wanted to make sure Coachella Valley products transported by train beat the competition to a hungry marketplace nationwide.

Coachella Valley Water District

Despite two World Wars, a stock market crash and the Great Depression, the single most defining occurrence in Indio's history was finding and keeping a water supply. When Chester A. Sparey arrived in Indio in 1915, many artesian wells had ceased to flow in the eastern end of the valley. The underground water table throughout the area was lowering and greater pump lists were being required.

Sparey was 26 years old in 1918 when the Coachella Valley Water District was formed and he joined its board of directors. Giving truth to Mark Twain's suggestion that "whiskey is for drinking and water is for fighting over," Sparey and the entire board were recalled in 1932 over water policy decisions that went all the way to Washington D.C.

Here's how Sparey recounted his story to *Indio Daily News* editor, Ole Nordland, in 1957:

I traveled to Indio in 1914 to survey and stake out the land I wanted to farm. I returned in 1915 aboard a boxcar loaded with lumber, fence materials, furniture and household goods, farm implements and a team of wild mules. It took nine months to get a well that went down 1,022 feet before hitting good water-bearing gravel.

In 1917, local attorney Thomas C. Yager called a group together to inform us that some men from San Diego intended to impound part of our local water supply, convey it by surface ducts to the lower end of the valley and sell it back to us. Using California statute, Yager laid out the formation of a County Water District to protect, conserve and augment our resources. Five members were elected to the first board. I represented Indio.

We retained a hydrology and geology expert from Los Angeles as our district engineer. He came by train for our monthly meetings. I would meet him in Indio at noon. After meetings, he had dinner at our house and we would spend the evening studying and going over our water problems until the midnight train for L.A.

By this time, Imperial Valley was already diverting the entire low flow of the Colorado River and needing more. We sent Yager to Washington D.C. on our behalf to speak with Secretary of the Interior, Franklin Lane. Legislation was passed and we kept Yager in Washington many months each year to represent our interests.

The key to us getting river water was the construction of a canal and storage system. We were working on that strategy when we were kicked out on our butts. Reasons for the recall were varied. Nevada-California Electric Power Co. feared losing revenue. Some wanted to keep the desert in its natural romantic state. Others feared overproduction of our out-of-season crops. Some with good wells felt they would survive the struggle for the last water hole. Some predicted that under full irrigation our climate would be changed - the valley would become a humid, torrid area and the date industry would be ruined.

We had guarded our natural supply because we didn't know if we'd ever get river water. We had opposed use of water in the lower valley for duck ponds and in the upper valley for golf courses. We lost the recall election. Yager died of a heart attack in 1931 at the young age of 47. He had just lived and worked too hard!

Ben Laflin, pictured here with his dog, was glad to have this artesian well on his property. Artesian pressure sent the water ten feet in the air. Steam engines needed water, and reliable wells were essential.

Chester A. Sparey, Coachella Valley Water District.

The Metropolitan Aqueduct

Public works projects designed to help lift the United States out of the Great Depression took center stage in the Indio of the 1930s. After all, the Coachella Valley stood between the raging Colorado River and the thirsty coastal communities of the Los Angeles Basin. The building of Boulder Dam and Parker Dam to its south brought construction of a new aqueduct to the mountains east of Indio. The first construction camp was raised at Fargo Canyon, east of Indio.

At the time, the aqueduct was the largest construction project in the world. It required an amount of steel equal to a full five months of the nation's production. The struggle to tunnel through the formidable Mount San Jacinto to get to the coast lasted nearly seven years. Work was completed at the West Portal of the San Jacinto Tunnel in 1939 with a nationwide radio broadcast.

Once the Metropolitan Aqueduct was finished, contracts were awarded to bring Colorado River irrigation water to the Coachella Valley via the All American Canal. That, observes local farmer and real estate investor Paul Ames, was a pivotal event in Indio's history. "I had just graduated from college when the canal opened. My granddad was a pioneer who came here in 1914 and worked the land. But we were pioneers, too. Everything we did with the canal water was new."

Paul Ames,
The Ames Group.

Bottom right, canal water distribution system construction began in 1948.

Photographs courtesy of Paul Ames.

Bringing Colorado River water into the valley, says Ames, gave agriculture the boost it needed to expand beyond a means to make a living into the largest industry in the valley.

With agriculture and tourism each being responsible for half a billion dollars in revenue to the Coachella Valley each year, Ames still sees a bright future for his vocation. "We've still got 70,000 acres of productive farm land left. We'll be farming in the valley for a long time to come."

By The Sea

A subject of discussion for decades, the Salton Sea is the largest inland lake in California and a significant stop for hundreds of bird species along the North American Flyway. The sea itself was created by human error. The Salton Sink is a natural geologic depression in the Earth's surface. The lowest point is more than 270 feet below sea level.

It's no wonder that, if the mighty Colorado River could form the Grand

Canyon, it could certainly overflow its banks and overtake a low-lying area like the Salton Sink. Geologists believe a great body of water once covered most of the Coachella Valley, extending north as far as Sacramento. A major seismic event thrust the land between here and the San Joaquin Valley up enough to form mountains, cutting off the waterway.

The land was still at or below sea level, and played host to ancient Lake

Date Palm Beach, circa 1950.

Records for the 1948 Speed Boat Regatta show that the Gold Cup Record was set by Guy Lombardo at 118.229 miles per hour.

Twenty-one world records were set at the Salton Sea Regatta.

The newspaper reported that Henry Kaiser, Jr., son of the famous industrialist, announced at a club meeting at the Hotel Indio prior to the 1949 Regatta that his father would enter two boats - "Hot Metal" and "Aluminum I."

Photographs courtesy of Paul Ames.

Cahuilla up to 500 years ago. As far back as 1815, salt was mined from the dry sink. In 1905, the Colorado River broke through a dike and filled the sink to an elevation of 195 feet, almost to the community of Mecca. Nowadays, Hoover Dam and the All American Canal control river flow.

Real estate entrepreneurs promoted the sea as a recreation spot that was "mysteriously enchanting and teeming with adventure" in the late 1920s. From the '30s well into the '50s, motor boat racers were drawn by what was reported to be the fastest water in the world - thanks to low barometric pressure and significant water density. During the World War II years, as many as 500 soldiers a day from nearby Camp Young descended on the Date Palm Beach Resort to swim. Even General Patton himself often visited.

Indio was the gateway to the Salton Sea for visitors coming from Los Angeles. The North Shore Yacht Club, opened in 1962, was described as a $2 million marine paradise with one of the largest marinas in Southern California. The Beach Boys, Jerry Lewis and the Marx Brothers were regulars at boating events and parties.

A Date With Destiny

"Honor your paternal aunt, the date palm, which was created out of the earth left over after the creation of Adam." - Prophet Muhammad

In 1886, C. P. Huntington, President of the Southern Pacific Railroad, brought date shoots back with him from a vacation in North Africa. He gave them to agriculturist, Pat Gale, who nurtured them. Sensing an opportunity, the U.S. Department of Agriculture sent a young explorer to Algeria around the turn of the century to study date culture and import offshoots for trial planting in the American Southwest.

The intrepid explorer returned with the conclusion that the Salton Basin was the most promising place in the U.S. for date culture. In 1901 and 1902, offshoots were imported from Egypt and the Persian Gulf. Bernard Johnson, who is often referred to as the "Father of the California Date Business," brought commercial date production to the American Southwest. He traveled repeatedly to the rugged countryside of French Algeria to bring the proper root stock for continued propagation.

The U. S. Department of Agriculture initiated an experimental date garden in 1904 near Mecca under Bernard Johnson's management. Most of the effort was moved to Indio in 1907 out of concern about the rising waters of the newly created Salton Sea, a large inland lake created by an

THE GREAT DATE

Date trees are among the oldest cultivated trees and are believed to have grown in North Africa for at least 8,000 years.

There are 60 references to date palms in the Old Testament. Dates were found buried with King Tutankhamen.

Date production is labor intensive. Female plants produce dates. One male tree is planted to pollinate 50 female trees. Commercial pollination is achieved by dusting the male pollen onto the female blooms one tree at a time. Date growers must climb each tree several times throughout the year to pollinate, cultivate and harvest the fruit.

Ben Laflin of Laflin Date Gardens took the good advice of his father, a Coachella Valley date pioneer, in crafting his business philosophy. He cites these simple rules for success that apply to virtually any business proposition:
One - Produce a quality product; Two - Bring what you grow to market profitably; Three - Don't farm from a distance; Four - Treat your workers well.

accidental breach in an agricultural dike meant to divert Colorado River water for irrigation. By the 1920s, Indio was established as the Date Capital of the U.S.

Women were a large part of the labor force when the fledgling date industry took off in the Coachella Valley. Leonhart Swingle recounts in a story published in a 1982 edition of the Coachella Valley Historical Society's *Periscope* that his wife commuted by the Southern Pacific Sidewinder train to her job at a packing house in Imperial Valley in 1919.

Much like the railroad's promotion of Indio as prime farmland, real estate developers sold the allure of Indio as an exotic destination in which to grow rich and grow dates. The truth of the matter was that date ranchers worked hard, often for little reward. Nevertheless, production continued to grow. By 1913, the Coachella Valley Date Growers Association had come into being, and packing houses were springing up around Indio.

Floyd Shields gave the otherwise homely date some sex appeal in 1924 with the opening of Shields Date Gardens on Highway 111. The promise of seeing "The Romance and Sex Life of the Date" in full Technicolor and sound lured people into the busy retail establishment for decades.

In the 1957 edition of Shields Date Gardens Coachella Valley Desert Trails guidebook, Mr. Shields is quoted as saying, "The natives of the Old World say: "A date palm must have its feet in the water and its head in the fires of heaven." I have lived on the Shields Date Gardens 37 winters and a thousand summers and I have seen the temperature hit 135 in the shade and 169 in the sun. In spite of this high temperature it might interest you to hear that we never perspire - but we do sweat like the devil - there is nothing fancy about it - it is just plain sweat!"

Even popular author, Zane Grey, succumbed to the allure of the date culture. His Flying Sphynx Ranch near Oasis included 20 acres of dates, a sprawling ranch and guesthouses and a landing field.

THE GREAT DATE

1924 - *The first Date Institute was held. The event was planned as an annual symposium to spread knowledge about dates both locally and throughout the world.*

1927 - *The Medjool date variety was introduced into the US with the arrival of 11 offshoots from Morocco.*

1934 - *The Deglet Noor Date Growers Association became the California Date Growers Association.*

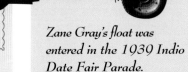

Zane Gray's float was entered in the 1939 Indio Date Fair Parade.

Staking a Claim

*Historic Mural: Historic Route 99,
Clark's Travel Center, corner of Indio
Boulevard and Sun Gold Street, artist
Duane Flatmo, completed in 1997.*

*Sun-Gold Date Gardens
and distinctive guest ranch
located on Highway 111
in Indio.*

Staking a Claim

From explorers arriving on horseback to fresh-faced homesteaders arriving by Iron Horse, the turn of the last century heralded a rush of activity in the American Southwest and especially in Indio. Gold fever hit in 1860 when the precious metal was discovered just east of the Colorado River. Mining came to the surrounding mountains. Present-day Mecca became a major freighting center and haven for prospectors.

Indio was thriving as a busy railroad settlement. The Southern Pacific Railroad kept sending boxcars loaded with Coachella Valley citrus and farm crops back to the Midwest with the promise that anyone buying desert land from the railroad would get free return passage to Indio. Plenty of dreamers took them up on their offer.

One of the first businessmen to capitalize on Indio's promise was A.G. Tingman. He came to town as a railroad construction boss and stayed long enough to become telegrapher and station agent. Sensing there were more than a few

A.G. Tingman with wife.

dollars to be made in the bustling trading post, he resigned his job in 1885 to open a general mercantile store.

A few years later, he became Indio's first postmaster. He continued to expand his small business empire with stables and corrals to provision freighters, prospectors and other fortune-seekers. Early pioneers remember Albert Tingman as an optimistic and warm-hearted man who was generous in praising others.

Southern Pacific Railroad car entering round house. Standing in front is Mrs. Edna Duncan, circa 1920. Photo courtesy of her daughter, Merle White.

Early Five & Dime store.

Ripple Date Gardens.

Business Boom

From 1885 to 1888, the land that wasn't earmarked for the railroad or the local Indian tribes was released for homesteading under the Desert Entry Act. In 1891, Tingman homesteaded and purchased 160 acres of Southern Pacific Railroad property. On it, he laid out the original Indio townsite. He sold lots and acreage while continuing to operate his store.

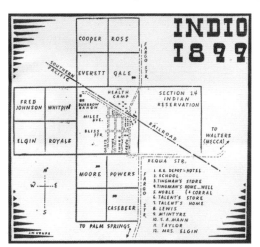

The Map of Indio Townsite, 1899, as featured on the cover of the 1992 *Periscope* from the Coachella Valley Historical Society, is said to have been drawn from notes and memories of Elizabeth Moore and son Otho. It shows the locations of houses, stores and important buildings, as well as the first property owners' names.

When A. G. Tingman sold his store in 1903, the townsite went with it. Two gentlemen by the names of Hunter and Pierce effectively bought downtown Indio and set out to seek their fortunes. Mr. Hunter was a sign painter by trade. He painted and placed street signs at every intersection. Many streets were named for Southern Pacific Railroad officials and early settlers.

Years later, in 1917, Henry McKay was appointed to oversee valley road improvements. He is credited with naming Indio's north-south roads spaced one mile apart for U.S. Presidents and the roads in between at the half-mile mark for U.S. Vice Presidents.

Right, Henry McKay named the Indio streets, early 1900s. Far right, "Saving Gasoline." Photo courtesy of Paul Ames.

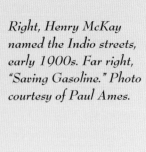

The Koehler Feed Store received the first official Indio business license in 1920. Fred Koehler and family moved to Indio in 1918 and he set up a transfer business, delivering feed to homesteaders by mule and wagon. After setting up shop with the feed store, Fred built the American Railway Express building, and his son, Francis, became its first agent. Francis Koehler was appointed constable of the Indio Township in 1924 and served in that position until 1944

In 1923, George and Marshall Peters opened Indio's first men's clothing store. They referred to their shop as the House of Quality, and proudly featured Arrow shirts, Stetson hats and Florsheim shoes. After the brothers died, Marshall's wife, Jean Malouf Peters, continued the clothing business as well as operating the Biltmore, one of Indio's finer hotels.

By 1925, Indio had grown into a bustling division headquarters for Southern Pacific with a twice-monthly payroll of nearly $14,000 pumping earnings back into the community. That year, nearly $200,000 was spent on new buildings in the business district. Construction included a bank, a theater, the Black Lumber Company building and a half dozen other structures named for their owners. The 80-room Hotel Indio was brand-new and owned by the Von der Ahe family who went on to establish the Von's grocery store chain.

In its heyday of the '30s, downtown Indio was full of busy hotels like Potter Hotel, the Plaza Hotel and Hotel Indio, where General George Patton often held court. By the beginning of the 21st Century, only Hotel Indio was still intact.

Koehler feed store, circa 1900's.

Early merchantile store.

Above left, Indio's first business license was for Koehler's Feed Store in 1930.

Hotel Indio, circa 1930.

A mule team of eight pulls freight wagon to the rear of H.E. Tallen's store in 1909.

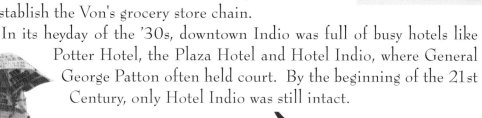

Southern California's thirst for water brought the next wave of business and commerce to Indio in the 1930s, with the building of the Metropolitan Aqueduct. Remote construction camps in the nearby mountains were full of miners and laborers with money in their pockets and nowhere to spend it except Indio.

This is how Mayor Harry Moore remembered those days:

"We had a devil of a flood in the mid-'30s and all the bridges — both railway and highway — were weakened. No truth or train could leave Indio. The aqueduct construction was going full force and 110 of their trucks with crewmembers were marooned in town. Besides, five passenger trains came in from the east, and none could leave the valley until the bridges were declared safe.

Jackhammer Café during a flood, circa 1930s.

We not only had the city to feed, but hundreds of aqueduct workers and hundreds more train passengers. Easterners got off the idled trains and flocked to the Jackhammer Café for a bit of "atmosphere." Even some of the ladies escorted by their husbands were frightened. When those brawny miners came up to the booths and demanded a dance, those women didn't dare refuse.

As mayor, I kept the city council in session the full time of our near-disaster. With food running short, it looked hopeless. To top it off, 150 vagrants, hungry as wolves were intent on taking the town over. Our police force was composed of only four men. I was ready to declare martial law when the first trucks of food came into Indio by way of the Palms to Pines Highway."

When a new batch of councilmen was sworn in, Mayor Moore had to address the existence of brothels on the "other side" of town. Moore told his colleagues that "the girls of our town wouldn't be safe even in the afternoon without these houses of ill-repute," and promptly took them on a tour of sin parlors known as Rosie's, Vi's, and Lightfoot's.

The councilmen found the brothels, but none of them was doing any business. There was an immediate reaction that the call houses might not be such a necessity and it was time to clean up the town. Then the mayor remembered the tour was conducted on the second Wednesday night of the month when all members of the aqueduct construction companies were required to stay in their respective camps for union meetings."

THE HOT SPOT

The Jackhammer Café on Jackson Street quickly became a nationwide legend as much for its décor as the antics that went on inside.

The café was built in the style of the early western saloons, with a long bar, dance floor, booths lining the walls and a mezzanine opening onto the main floor.

The Jackhammer became the Hawaiian Club in 1945, and the building was converted to a Western Auto Supply.

Japanese Families

An exclusion order in 1942 was issued requiring all local Japanese residents to be evacuated. Elmer Suski was one of the evacuees forced to leave businesses, homes, farms and crops that were ready to harvest with no

First generation Indio residents, left to right, Seoti Nagata, Nui Nagata, Hiroshi Sakai, Mura Sakemi, Toyoighi, Shizuyo Shibata, Hikotaro Nagata and Ai Nagata.

advance notice. He recalls that many non-Japanese farming families offered their support to save the crops. The Westerfield family, in charge of the Coachella First National Bank, was instrumental in keeping the farms going and depositing the money collected from crops into the Japanese families' accounts in their absence.

Even though some had lived in their homes for 36 years, the Japanese left without resentment. Upon their return, ads were placed in the *Date Palm* newspaper expressing thanks to "businessmen, teachers, ministers, and law

enforcement agencies for demonstrating a true understanding of the democracy under which we have enjoyed privileges and protection unknown in any other country in the world."

In the meantime, Army soldiers, tanks and equipment had begun arriving by the trainload in the spring of 1942 for the Desert Training Center, headquartered at Camp Young north of the town of Desert Center. The training center, which spanned 16,000 square miles of California, Arizona and Nevada, was under the command of Major General George S. Patton, who led a tank corps in France during World War I. Patton was preparing troops to fight in the harsh desert conditions of North Africa.

Nagata family left to right, mother Nui, father Seitaro, daughters Amy Musashi, Grace Musashi, Lily Shimiza and baby George on lap.

WAR DECLARED

In 1941, when World War II was declared by Franklin Roosevelt, 16 air raid posts were established in the Coachella Valley, and a local drum and bugle corps was started. Local Japanese residents swore their allegiance to the United States, turning in guns, radios, Samurai swords and boxes of Japanese books to officials. Indio's Japanese vegetable farmers were put under protective supervision by the federal government so they could continue to serve as food producers for the war effort. Many Japanese workers, who were able-bodied but ineligible to serve in the military, moved into the valley to replace Mexican farm workers who had gone off to war.

Some of the young men left camps to volunteer for the U.S. Army. Locals Tom Sakemi, Kuz Nagata, Sus and Sam Musashi all received the purple heart.

Shirley Butvidas and Cherry Ishimatsu, circa 1970.

Bank of America, circa 1930.

The U.S. government leased 500 acres to develop nurseries to grow guayale plants from Mexico for production of rubber for the military.

In the spring of 1943, Coachella Valley Union High School listed 179 alumni in the Armed Forces.

When the Desert Training Center was closed in 1944, Italian POWs did the dismantling process.

General Patton and his troops.

Camp Young Begins Operations

Harold Taylor was manager of the Indio branch of the Bank of America when Camp Young began operations. Money for the Army payroll arrived in Indio by train as registered mail. Military personnel would meet at the station in armored vehicles, receive the money and accompany Taylor to the Indio Post Office on Fargo Street. He recalls the highest payroll paid out in one day was $3.5 million.

Bank of America staff and customers, including Branch Manager Harold Taylor, Assistant Manager Tom Mullan and customer Jackie Cochran (top center).

The regular routine called for Taylor to sign for the money, which was then transported to the bank. The money came in bags two feet wide and three feet high. Each bag was taken into the vault and counted out for distribution to each Army unit in the command. Finance officers for each unit arrived at the bank with armed carriers. Guards were stationed along Miles Avenue, Fargo Street and Smurr Street.

In 1934 Tom Mullan moved to Indio to take a job with Bank of America. He lived in Indio for 62 years until his death in 1996 and worked for the bank for 48 years.

This excerpt from "Mullan It Over," a book of Tom's recollections was published by his wife, Madeline Flynn Mullan in 1997.

What Indio Was Like in the 1940s?

In the early '40s, Indio's business district consisted of more than 125 businesses including, of course, our bank, two weekly newspapers, a mortuary, a motion picture theater, two modern hospitals, five hotels and apartments, courts and auto camps, as well as two department stores and grocery stores.

Throughout the years, many Hollywood celebrities came into the bank inquiring about land available for agriculture or development, including Desi Arnaz and the Marx Brothers. Gary Cooper's brother was manager of Coachella Valley Savings and Loan. He was interested in Salton Sea property, as were Phil Harris and Jerry Lewis.

Camp Young held 25,000 soldiers at a time, which translated to 2,500 soldiers in Indio. There was one theatre, a few restaurants and a tiny department store. Many soldiers had Sunday or holiday dinners with residents.

The Desert Training Center became the largest Army post in the world.

Major General George Patton and his staff were inducted into the local chapter of the Veterans of Foreign Wars (V.F.W.) for servicemen. Sports programs were launched at night-lighted ball fields in Indio and Coachella.

Hoods were placed on all railroad signals and train headlights in case of air raid blackouts. The Army built Thermal Airport to support operations at Camp Young.

The War Production Board approved development of the Iron Chief Mine at Eagle Mountain, 45 miles east of Indio, along with a $50 million steel plant in Fontana, California.

Indio local celebrity, Jacqueline Cochran was named Director of Women Pilots of the U.S. Army Air Force. She trained women flyers to ferry Hudson bombers between the United States and England.

Above, General Patton (center) and General McNair (right) at the Desert Training Center.

Female pilots were deactivated in 1944, but Jackie Cochran continued to serve as a special consultant to the Army Air Force.

As a Captain, Ralph Pawley (son of Judge Pawley) served in the medical section of General Douglas MacArthur's headquarters for the U.S. Armed Forces in the Southern Pacific. He returned stateside as a Major.

Modern-Day Desert Pioneers

The post-war years were marked by the achievements of a new wave of modern-day desert pioneers. Many of them were the next generation of early founding families whose roots were already planted in Indio. Some of them went on to raise families, create businesses and distinguish themselves in the community and beyond.

Left to right, Ray and Sophie Arriola, daughters Becky Hernandez, Cindy Townley and granddaughter Andra Jenkins.

In 1963, Heimark became the Budweiser distributor in the valley with half a dozen employees and two trucks. When asked what the key to success was for his family's business, Gene Heimark says, "If it wasn't for General Patton and luck, the business might never have taken off."

Shirley Butvidas standing next to her plane at the Indio Airport. The Desert Bats, headquartered at the Indio Airport, flew weekly "breakfast flights."

Herlindo Arriola was farming watermelon, corn and carrots in the valley in 1927. As a side job, he and his wife, Euilia, made Mexican bread and hand-tossed tortillas in their humble home on Oasis Street. They supplied the downtown Indio drug store and dozens of regular customers, using corn from local farmers.

Ray Arriola was born in Indio in 1930 and owns the family business that still serves a faithful clientele looking for fresh corn tortillas and chips along with salsa and tamales. He remembers, at age six, being assigned the task of keeping the engine of his dad's Model T Ford throttled so it would run a rubber fan belt attached to a hand-operated corn grinder. The strange contraption helped the family increase production to meet growing demand. Parts of the corn-grinding machine are still in use.

Rudy Heimark started Heimark Distributing after Prohibition ended in the early '30s. He was trucking locally grown tomatoes to the Los Angeles market when downtown Indio bar owners began asking him to haul "Eastside Beer" back with him on the return trip. He stored the beer in the garage of his home on Miles and Park Avenue, launching a wholesale beer business.

It wasn't long before he opened Rudy's Liquor at the corner of Highway 99 and Jackson (which is now Indio Boulevard and Fargo Street) near the railroad tracks. Rudy's son, Gene, remembers troops headed for training camps hopping off the train, running like crazy to the liquor store, throwing down a $20 bill for a half-pint and racing back to the train (often without their change) as the train rolled out of the station.

Lucille Tune Cavanaugh came to the valley with her family in 1930. Her father helped built Highway 74 from Palm Desert into the mountains and the road from Indio to Blythe, which became Interstate 10. Lucille married fellow Coachella Valley High School graduate, Frank Cavanaugh, in 1937. Frank started his own business - Cavanaugh Electric - in 1946 on Fargo Street. The store sold appliances and was one of the first electrical contractors in the valley. In the late 1950s, Frank built his own building on Highway 111. Cavanaugh Electric and Air Conditioning is still serving customers today with son Rod at the helm.

Shirley Dillan Butvidas became manager of the Indio Airport in the late 1940s, when the facility was located on north Jackson Street on land known as Jewell Park.

The U.S. government made flying lessons available to returning servicemen, and the Indio Flying Service conducted ground and flight training. One of the young men to go through the training program was

Peter Butvidas. He and Shirley were married and stayed in Indio to raise their family. As a tax accountant, Peter served for many years on the board of the Indio Chamber of Commerce and the Indio City Council. Shirley volunteered for numerous community causes and, now in her 80s, continues to live in Indio and support organizations like California Women for Agriculture and the Coachella Valley Boys and Girls Club.

Yellow Mart got its start as Indio War Surplus, in the 1940s selling short supply items (jackets, blankets and bed sheets) out of a Quonset hut on Indio Boulevard. When the war ended, Dick Friestad and his brothers Russ and John bought and expanded the store to offer more clothing, tents, hardware and camping gear.

Yellow Mart started as Indio War Surplus.

Business continued to boom thanks in part to the government-sponsored Braceros program that brought farm workers from across the border at Calexico. Mercantile buses brought ranch workers to town so they could cash paychecks, buy merchandise and send money home. Dick recalls preparing the money orders and taking them to the Post Office. The following week when the Braceros returned, he'd give them their mailing receipts.

In 1956, the store became Yellow Mart. It continued to evolve to meet the needs of local customers adding fishing tackle for the Salton Sea, guns and ammunition for dove and duck hunting, western wear for equestrians and rodeo competitors, and sporting goods for adult and Little League baseball.

June Hall's father was among the early pioneers of tourism at the Salton Sea. He and a wealthy partner set out to create an Egyptian-theme resort complete with pyramid. When the financier gave up, June's father persevered alone, building Date Palm Resort. As June remembers, those were glory days at the sea, with crystal-clear water and miles of pristine beaches.

June met her husband, Sgt. Cameron Hall, on the beach, where the handsome young soldier was taking some leisure time with friends. They were married within a year and returned to Indio to raise their family once his military service was over.

A major effort to establish the Salton Sea as a prime sport fishing location was started in 1948. After two years of trying to introduce one species at a time, a decision was made to plant every popular fish variety that could be netted out of the Gulf of California. Fish were transported by tank truck to the Salton Sea.

In Good Faith

Places of worship have always been important to Indio residents. A variety of faiths have been represented to serve the community's needs.

The Coachella Valley Christian Church began on Easter Sunday, April 1, 1923. A Sunday school had already been organized at the Oasis School. When the desks became too small for the older children, church leaders borrowed two dozen folding chairs from the Christian Missionary Society of Southern California.

Above, African Methodist Episcopal Church on Date Street. At right, Our Lady of Perpetual Help Catholic Church.

The original church was in Coachella. As the congregation grew, it looked for bigger space. To pay for the effort, church members baked cakes, pies and date bars, and sold them each year from a booth at the Date Festival.

In April of 1930, Reverend L.W. Minor founded the African Methodist Episcopal in Indio. In 1977, when Reverend Carolyn Tyler became pastor, she did so as the first woman to be ordained an Itinerant Elder in the 52-year history of the A.M.E.'s Southern California Conference.

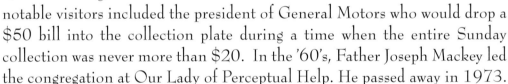

Tom Mullan chaired the meeting in 1936 which led to the building of the first Catholic Church in Indio. Mullan recounted that several famous people frequented the church in the early days, such as film stars Loretta Young and Irene Dunne. Other notable visitors included the president of General Motors who would drop a $50 bill into the collection plate during a time when the entire Sunday collection was never more than $20. In the '60's, Father Joseph Mackey led the congregation at Our Lady of Perceptual Help. He passed away in 1973.

The Foursquare Gospel Church in Indio began as an independent institution under pastor Jewel Brown, and was brought into the Foursquare organization in 1957.

The Chapel at FitzHenry Funeral Home on Requa Street was originally a multidenominational church built in 1921, which later became a Methodist Church. The FitzHenry Family bought it in 1955 and converted it into a mortuary as the first of their valley locations. Jim FitzHenry was born and raised in Indio and remembers it as a great place to grow up "Everything you needed was within a two-block radius downtown," he says.

Today, people of many faiths worship and enjoy fellowship in Indio. Even "snowbirds" have a place to practice their faith, thanks to ordained minister Dick Schroeder, who also is the Director of the Indio Senior Center. The vehicle resorts provide meeting places for nondenominational church services. He estimates at the height of the season his gathering attracts up to 1,100 people on any given Sunday. Says Schroeder, "Like the swallows returning to Capistrano, our snowbirds come back year after year. They come because they love desert winters, the Coachella Valley identifies a lifestyle and they like seeing their seasonal friends each year."

The Chapel at FitzHenry Funeral Home on Requa Street.

Hub Of The Valley

Indio was a well-rounded community in its own right, advertising itself in a 1959 scenic guide map as the "Hub of the California Desert Playground." The brochure enticed readers with this promise - "Indio is not a tourist resort dependent upon a fast profit in a short season. It has a solid economy built on agriculture, distribution of goods and services and some light-to-medium manufacturing. Indio is a real All-American town where prices and rates are realistic and there is no such thing as a tourist tab. We like it that way and hope you do, too."

Indio was proud of its cultural assets that offered residents of all ages ample opportunities to get involved and enrich themselves. In the late 1950s, 46 service and social organizations were listed by the Chamber of Commerce ranging from Beta Sigma Phi Sorority to Wild Game Propagation Club to the Women's Christian Temperance Union.

The Coachella Valley Community Concert Association, organized in 1950, boasted a membership of 800 people in the late '60s, presenting four concerts each year. Des Arts, organized in 1963, was Indio's association of active artists.

Indio Municipal Band, organized in 1965, was comprised of professional businessmen and women, housewives and students.

Recreational activities were also plentiful in the growing community. Indio Municipal Golf Course was, and still is, the only night-lighted course in the valley. Golfers could enjoy a clubhouse, driving range, coffee shop and pro shop. The Indio Bowl was a busy 24-lane bowling facility that hosted league bowling five nights a week.

The Coachella Valley Recreation and Park District came into existence in 1951. By the '60s, it operated the Pawley Pool daily to the public from June to September. Known as the coolest spot in town, the swim center took in 14,000 admissions in a typical season. It also supervised the training of the CorVina Swim Team and Synchronized Swim Team.

Throughout the year, the District also presented flag football and basketball programs, church volleyball leagues, tennis and badminton, oil painting, arts and crafts, knitting, guitar lessons, cake decorating, karate, ballet, baton, dog obedience, and much more.

The Coachella Valley Boys' Club in Indio was dedicated on March 17, 1968. It cost $170,000 to build with donated labor, private fundraising and a grant of $27,500 from the Bob Hope Desert Classic golf tournament. Its Date Street location behind Jackson Street Park attracted 1,200 members the first year who logged in 67,000 visits to the center.

Supplement to The Press, *and* The Daily Enterprise, *Tuesday, September 8, 1964 .*

John P. Carroll, Coachella Valley Boys Club, receives plaque from Bob Hope, 1968.

MANUFACTURING FIRMS

The 1968 *Indio Community Profile* published by the Chamber of Commerce and the City, listed a diverse group of "Manufacturing Firms" representing a variety of activities doing business in and around the area:

California Date Growers
Coachella Valley Ice
Brad Thompson, Industries
Richard A. Glass Company
Massey Sand and Rock
Palco Linings, Inc.
Safeway Pre-Pakt Produce
Tom Sakai Produce
WEMS, Inc.
Meredith, Simpson & York
Bermite Powder
Seven-Up Bottling Company
Carr and Carr Bulk Plant
Wood Specialties Company
Culligan Soft Water Service

Above right, Daily News, Monday, December 27, 1965.

At right, Valley Sanitation District.

INDIO AMONG TOP 10 IN GROWTH

Road Sla[...]ter Record Set

Research Findings Unveiled

By DOROTHY WATSON
City Editor

ACCIDENTS CLAIM 832
By United Press International

Head-On Collision

Early Efforts Pay Off

It was during the 1960s and '70s that "urban renewal" became "redevelopment." Cities everywhere were cashing in on government funds from the U.S. Department of Housing and Urban Development to refurbish or reclaim land that was not meeting its current potential.

Utilities and infrastructure are critical to the growth of every community. Without adequate public services like water, sewer, telephone and electricity, no community can sustain itself and prosper.

In 2005 Valley Sanitary District marks its 80th year of operation. Current board member, Bill Teague, worked for the public agency for 30 years before retiring and being elected to the governing board. The agency was born as Indio Sanitary District in 1925, just two years after legislation passed to provide for such districts.

Says Teague, "I'm stilled amazed by the insight those early community leaders exhibited. They wanted the services but didn't have much money. So they appointed block captions in every neighborhood where sewer lines were set to be installed. The block captions organized their neighborhoods to provide most of the labor digging the trenches for pipes to be laid." Teague is equally optimistic about the future. He believes the District is "blessed" with a strong elected board of community leaders and successful businesspeople as well as a trained staff that understands the importance of master-planning for the future.

The 1969 Indio Chamber of Commerce brochure calls Indio's residential offerings "Luxury Living under the Palms," stating, "Indio's natural setting amid sprawling date gardens lends itself to gracious living. Tasteful architecture is the natural expression of a desire to live inexpensively yet luxuriously, evident in the abundance of ranch-style homes and typical California desert dwellings set back on residential streets lined with marching palms, row after row. Attractive three- and four-bedroom homes range from $13,000 to $30,000 and more. Apartments rent from $55 to $175 per month."

Thanks to California's ambitious freeway construction frenzy in the 1960s, the car was king and motor court hotels were all the rage. The Hyatt Thunderbird Motor Hotel on Highway 86 advertised itself as having 70 beautifully appointed suites, three heated pools, a steak house and coffee shop. The Indio Hacienda, the largest luxury motor hotel with 123 spacious air conditioned rooms, featured a giant Olympic size heated pool and a smaller pool for children. The Hacienda was located on Interstate 10. Today it is known as the Best Western Date Tree Hotel and is located on Indio Boulevard.

Indio residents didn't have to go far to buy a car, with four dealerships representing all American auto manufacturers along Highway 99. Max McCandless was the original dealer of General Motors products. Ben Cowan started his Ford dealership in downtown Indio and relocated to Highway 99 in the 1950s. Kay Olsen's Imperial Motors was the Chrysler dealer, and Doc Gurley ran Valley Motors, featuring the Chevrolet and Oldsmobile brands.

Mike Burns bought the Ford franchise in 1966 and renamed it Fiesta Ford. He remembers going to Indio City Hall in the 1980s to discuss ways to upgrade and enhance Highway 99's Auto Row. The discussions continued into the 1990s, when a decision was made to look for property for a new concept — an Auto Mall opened in 1999. Says Mike, "The County expected it to take 10 to 12 years for them to get their investment back. We paid them back in five. Needless to say, the freeway location has been a tremendous success."

Sambo's Pancake House & Coffee Shop, Highway 10.

Hotel Potter and Ames Real Estate on Fargo and Tingman Street.

Left at top, Miles Avenue in the Sun Gold development on the cover of the 1969 Indio Chamber brochure. Left middle, homes along Bliss Avenue, 1969. Left bottom, home of Mrs. Merle White in Boe-Del Heights, circa 1970.

Early auto dealers on Highway 99.

Destinations

Like many immigrants in the early days of the 20th Century, John Peters' parents came to America in search of a dream. As a child, John remembers wondering why his family would trade their arid homeland of Lebanon for the equally desolate desert landscape of Indio. Nevertheless, when Peters spent $500,000 in 1962 to build a motor hotel complex on Miles Avenue, he adopted Indio's Arabian theme and called it El Morocco.

A precursor to the destination resorts of today's Palm Springs Desert Resort Communitites, El Morocco featured an on-site beauty shop, barber shop, travel agency, cocktail lounge and supper club. When Peters served as president of the Indio

El Morroco on Miles Avenue, the desert's newest motor hotel, opened December, 1963.

Chamber of Commerce and spent one term as an Indio City Councilman, he floated the idea of changing Indio's name to something more "upscale" like "Rancho Indio" or "Indio Palms." No agreement could be reached and the idea failed.

Two weeks after the venerable El Morocco closed in 1987, George Bishop opened Cactus Jack's restaurant on Highway 111. Half a dozen former El Morocco employees went to work at the new eatery. One of them, night chef Rafael Calderon, is still there.

In 1972, an *Indio Daily News* headline proclaimed, "Indio Assumes New Role as Industrial and Commercial Center." The article went on to report that "the annual statement of the State Board of Equalization show that Indio taxable sales now exceed those of Redlands and El Centro."

Karen Oppenheim was publisher of the *Daily News* for nearly 10 years beginning in 1979. She had come from *The Detroit News*, which at the time had the largest evening newspaper circulation in the county, so the newspaper in Indio was a big chance for her.

As she recounts, "Good newspaper people are the same everywhere and the staff in Indio was terrific." They were obviously also talented, since the *Daily News* was named best newspaper in the state in its circulation category two years in a row in 1985 and 1986 by the California Newspaper Publishers Association.

$100 Million Subdivision To Rise In Indio

BY JERI TAYLOR, DAILY NEWS STAFF WRITER

A record shattering flight was monitored from its swimming pool; the nation's foremost women golfers teed off from its greens; the world's most elusive millionaire was a frequent guest, and one day both the President of the United States and the general who preceded him in office dropped in for a chat.

Long responsible for placing Indio on the map among the greats of government, aviation, science, politics and the movie world, has been the prestigious Cochran-Odlum Ranch. A private home and working ranch for the past 30-plus years, development is now underway toward the creation of more than 3,000 condominiums and single-family dwellings, plus a country club, golf course and tennis complex.

But this $100 million subdivision all started with a flat tire. Early in their respective careers, Floyd Odlum, financier and industrialist, and Jacqueline Cochran, aviatrix and businesswoman, were driving through the Coachella Valley. They had a flat tire somewhere near the present ranch. The couple purchased the barren desert in 1935 at about $100 per acre.

Floyd Odlum conducted the major portion of his far-reaching business enterprises from the ranch, and associates became accustomed to talking over million-dollar negotiations at an umbrella table in the garden, as Odlum rarely worked at a desk. To escape the crippling effects of rheumatoid arthritis, it was even more likely that his negotiations took place in their Olympic-sized swimming pool where, sporting a baseball cap, dark glasses and swim trunks, the "Miracle Man of Finance" floated around on two rubber rings for four hours a day, in touch with the nerve centers of the world by telephone.

A $3,346,140 building permit, the largest ever issued by the City of Indio, is signed and picked up by developers of the new Indio fashion mall which includes Harris' department store on Highway 111 near Monroe. Seen here issuing permit is Terisa Smith, building department clerk, while V. Nicholas Gisotti, center, project coordinator for FHM Investments, and Ernest P. Howard, project architect, fill out necessary papers in Indio City Hall yesterday.

Staff Photo - Indio Daily News – 1979

Fruits Of Their Labor

Jens Harboe was a man of many talents - real estate developer, civic leader and consummate Indio business booster. During the late 1960s and early 1970s, Harboe became one of the town's biggest cheerleaders and pitchman.

In his Harboe Valley Letter, a promotional piece for his real estate business, Jens suggested that departing American Airlines passengers at Palm Springs Airport be given a gift of locally grown grapefruit. The Indio Chamber's Agriculture Committee embraced the idea. They set out to create a high-visibility public relations campaign. In keeping with the times, the group looked to Miss Indio and her court to act as ambassadors for the program.

Jens' wife, Ellen, designed and made grapefruit-yellow costumes for the girls that were accessorized with

Photos courtesy of Jens Harboe.

Among the bevy of Grapefruit Girls were Palm Springs Mayor Frank Bogert's daughter, Donna, and Ben and Pat Laflin's daughter, Barbara.

The Grapefruit Girls with Chuck Conners.

jaunty billed hats and go-go boots. A dozen attractive young ladies were on deck at the airport each Saturday and Sunday to hand out drawstring plastic bags of grapefruit to passengers boarding planes for Chicago. The bags contained two plump grapefruit along with a promotional piece featuring the valley's many attractions, inviting the traveler to "Come Back to the Coachella Valley."

The Grapefruit Girls also made public appearances and posed for photos with celebrities. In an effort to show that grapefruit was more than just a breakfast drink, the Chamber teamed up with Oasis Gardens and Pepe Lopez Tequila to deliver "Coachella Coolers" to travel agents in town for industry meetings and conventions.

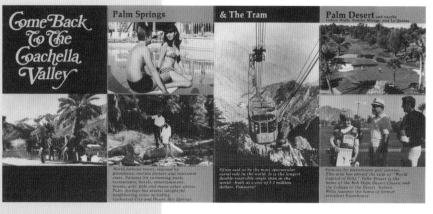

In The Mood

Jens Harboe wasn't done just yet. He enlisted the help of famous bandleader and musician, Fred Waring, to write a song for his hometown. "Mood Indio" was dedicated to Bob Allen, Manager, and the Indio Chamber of Commerce.

Mood Indio

I'm in that mood Indio
It's a mood you should know
Cause it's the mood of a city on the go!

Better start making plans
Don't lose out on your chance
To have a date with the city of romance.

You'll have that feel of success
With minimum stress - casual dress
Avoid that big city mess
Choose your town - don't settle for less.

I wouldn't have missed it
See if you can resist it
It's the loveliest town I know
It's the town with that mood Indio.

Miss Coachella Valley Grapefruit, Racquel Welch, with Paul Ames, president of the Grapefruit Advisory Board, circa 1960.

The song Mood Indio was written in 1969 by Fred Waring and Jens Harboe, past president of the Indio Chamber of Commerce.

Below left, the Grapefruits Girls hold a "Mood Indio" banner with Jens Harboe, Chamber of Commerce President and Bob Allen, manager of the Chamber of Commerce, circa 1970.

Landmark Golf Company

One person who certainly got into the Mood Indio spirit in the 1990s was Ernie Vossler, President of Landmark Golf Company. He opened Landmark Golf Club in Indio in November of 1999 with 36 holes of championship

The Skins Game 2001 at Landmark Golf Club. Left to right, Colin Montgomerie, Greg Norman, Jesper Parnevik and Tiger Woods.

golf, a full-service clubhouse, and a practice range. Landmark Golf Club brought national attention to Indio as the home of The Skins Game from 1999 to 2002.

The nationally televised event featured top-seeded golfers like Mark O'Meara, Fred Couples, Sergio Garcia, David Duval, Colin Montgomerie, Vijay Singh, Jesper Parnevik, Phil Mickelson and Tiger Woods. In the 2001 outing, Greg Norman walked away with the whole $1 million purse while viewers from across the country got an eyeful of Indio as a vacation destination and great place to live

Says Vossler, "In the late 1990s, the City of Indio offered an attractive combination of conditions and opportunities for development of a successful golf community. Indio was, and still is, in the path of major rapid economic growth. The City Council and staff wanted responsible development, and they were cooperative to work with in accomplishing our mutual goals. The price of land worked for development, and there was a community need for challenging championship golf."

"The land we were drawn to," Vossler continues, "already had flood control to the north and a water source-irrigation canal running through the property providing function and aesthetics. And the bonus was The Skins Game, an internationally recognized television marketing tool, was looking for a host site. Indio was the ideal place at that time for Landmark Golf Company to embark on developing a remarkable golf community."

The Skins Game 2001 at Landmark Golf Club in Indio. From left to right, Joe Walser, Jr., Landmark; Ernie Vossler, Landmark; Greg Norman; Judy Vossler, Tournament Director; Robert Wagner, Landmark celebrity host.

The Skins Game Pro-Am 1999, left to right, Robert Wagner, William Devane and Johnny Pott, three-time Ryder Cup Team.

Justice For All

Indio emerged as a second seat of government for Riverside County with the 1968 opening of a $2.3 million four-story administrative building on Highway 111 and Oasis Street. The high-rise building was a landmark in its day, providing a single location for a wide variety of county service agencies useful to valley residents.

Within its thoroughly modern architecture of the '60s, the center housed offices of the County Assessor, Agriculture, Building and Safety, Public Defender and District Attorney, County Schools, Sheriff's Department, County Clerk, Probation Department, Disaster Preparedness, Planning Commission, Public Health, and quarters for the Municipal and Superior courts.

By the early 1990s, Riverside County staff and services had outgrown the administrative center. Officials were concerned that outdated security measures were allowing prisoners in custody to be brought through the same public entrance as potential jurors. Short on funding and long on bureaucratic red tape, officials were forced to find a creative solution to their expansion needs.

Taking a very innovative approach, then Riverside County Supervisor Patricia "Corky" Larson structured a financing plan using court fees, redevelopment monies and various county funds. Desert Facilities Corporation, a private, nonprofit entity was brought in to build a jail and courthouse complex next door to the administrative building as a joint venture with the County.

Palm Springs architect Donald A. Wexler, well-known for his mid-century modern aesthetic, designed the Larson Justice Center,

Patricia "Corky" Larson

pictured above. The project was unprecedented for being finished on time and under budget. As a testament to her resolve in spearheading the project, the facility was named after Patricia "Corky" Larson.

WORKFORCE DEVELOPMENT CENTER

In 1988, College of the Desert began offering classes at Indio High School to make course work more accessible to residents of the east valley. In the 1990s, officials from College of the Desert, the City of Indio and Riverside County worked together to create a "one-stop" education center on the site of a former department store on Monroe Street.

The result is a facility that houses not only College of the Desert's Eastern Valley Center but myriad other agencies including a Workforce Development Center, Department of Public Social Services, State of California Department of Rehabilitation, Employment Development Department, and Riverside County Economic Development Agency.

The mission of the Workforce Development Center is to provide job seekers with education, job training, and employment programs.

In The Zone

In 1991, the Coachella Valley Enterprise Zone was designated by the state to include most of the commercial and industrial land in Indio. The Desert Communities Empowerment Zone was created to complement the state's incentives with federal tax credits, making Indio one of only a few locations in the country with both an Enterprise Zone and Empowerment Zone.

The zones are economic development tools to offer financial and tax incentives to encourage business growth and job creation within specific geographical areas. Clusters of golf-related companies, wood shutter and furniture manufacturers, and nationally known industry outlets located in Indio have taken advantage of the employee hiring credits and other services. Since the Zone's inception, thousands of new jobs have been realized.

One of the Zone's major success stories is Guy Evans Inc., a company specializing in custom doors, millwork and hardware. Guy Evans started as a carpenter working out of his pick-up truck. His Indio showroom and warehouse set to open in 2005 will be the centerpiece of his company that

employs over 300 people with offices in Las Vegas, Riverside and a future one in San Diego.

Guy Evans, Inc. has grown 1000% in the last decade by securing long-term contracts with several regional and national developers to provide custom construction products. Guy not only sees his business future in Indio, he lives in Indio as well. Says Evans, "My company has to be in the right place — and that place is Indio."

Coachella Valley Enterprise Zone

CVEZ was chartered in 1991 and is one of 39 Zones in California. The Zone is 56 miles square and encompasses the cities of Indio and Coachella, and the unincorporated areas of Thousand Palms, Thermal and Mecca. Nearly 70 Indio businesses have taken advantage of financial incentives to hire employees since the Zone was created.

Since 1991, over 10,000 new jobs in over 400 companies have come on line in the Coachella Valley as a direct result of Zone incentives. Nearly 7,000 jobs were created in 2004 alone, generating more than $70 million in employer savings.

Indio Chamber of Commerce Presidents

1921	Roy Pawley	1971	John Gossett
1936	L.W. Thurlow	1972	E. Van Gortel
1937	E.G. Shepard	1974	John Ivey
1944	E.W. Johnston	1975	Med Jeansonne
1945	Ned Williams	1977	Thomas Hunt
1946	Ralph Crom	1978	Dick Jandt
1947	Harry Whittlesey	1979	Andy Sfingi
1948	Bill Becker	1980	Merritt Wiseman
1949	Roger Hand	1981	Paul Ames
1951	James Young	1982	Jean Mullenax
1951	Guy Brubaker	1983	Bob Testa
1952	Harry Holt	1984	Gene Heimar
1954	Allen Willard, Sr.	1985	Rudy Acosta
1955	Roy King	1986	Bob Williams
1956	James Wright	1987	Richard Friestad
1957	Arthur Ahrens	1989	Bill Carr
1958	Ira Johnson	1990	Art Torres
1958	Clarence Washburn	1991	Lucille Swain
1959	Norman FitzHenry	1992	Phillip Hawes
1960	Arthur Cooper	1993	Michael Savage
1961	Dr. George Mason	1994	Bill Proctor
1962	E.F. Pearson	1995	Mick Barnhill
1963	John Slater	1996	Bill Northrup
1964	Phil Ault	1997	Doug York
1965	John Peters	1999	Rick Trinchero
1966	James J. O'Brien	2000	Ron Hare
1968	Elmer Suski	2002	PJ Gillespie
1969	Peter Butvidas	2004	Dr. Frank Curry
1970	Jens Harboe	2005	Dr. Frank Curry
1970	Mike Burns		

Miss Indio cuts the ribbon as Indio Chamber of Commerce and City officials look on during the grand opening of Von's supermarket in July of 1970.

Indio Chamber of Commerce parade float, Elmer Suski, Mark Levine, Bob Allen, circa 1960.

Chamber of Commerce

The Indio Chamber of Commerce serves as the Visitors Center for the City of Indio and actively promotes the community to tourists and visitors. Through its economic development programs, the Chamber responds to inquiries from businesses looking to locate to the area.

One of the great sagas of the old west took place in the early 20th Century in the Coachella Valley--the transformation of the arid Salton Sink into rich winter gardens of early vegetables, lush date and citrus groves and acres of early grapes. Farmers and farm workers fought sun, wind, sand, dust and most of all, unending summer heat to make the desert bloom. Well water was supplemented, after 1950, by Colorado River water brought in by a branch of the All-American Canal.

Sewing Seeds

Historical Mural: History of Agriculture, corner of Towne Street and Miles Avenue, artist Jim Fanestock, completed 2002.

*Date palm grove
in Indio.*

Sewing Seeds

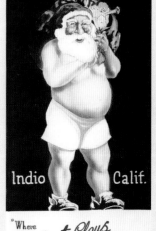

Early Indio postcard.

Over the years, Indio has been a plum many people have wanted to pick. Each has sewn his own seeds for the future of the community. Some became famous, others notorious. Most received little or no recognition at all. Legions of hard-working everyday people contributed to Indio's longevity. Together, they built a community from bits and pieces of their own personalities and talents.

Local author and educator, Pat Laflin, says it best in her pictorial history of the Coachella Valley: "The story of Indio is a story of how communities come into being. Reading early newspapers, one can sense the flavor of life here – before incorporation, before water systems and electricity, before paved roads, before firemen and hospitals – a decent life depended on ordinary people doing extraordinary things to care for one another."

Like many of her contemporary Indio pioneers, Mrs. Florence Sparey echoed their sentiments when she said, "It is amazing that so many of us came here to farm, and we ended up doing everything else but farm." What the early settlers did accomplish, however, was sowing the seeds of a stable community for future generations to enjoy.

Early aerial view of a growing community.

School Days

There were eight elementary schools in the Coachella Valley in 1930. Roosevelt School in Indio graduated 30 eighth graders that year, including George Sakemi. At last count, Desert Sands Unified School District listed nine elementary schools, three middle schools and two high schools in Indio alone, with more facilities on the drawing boards. Coachella Valley Unified School District is also growing to keep pace with the needs of Indio's families.

The first Indio Grammar School was built in 1898 of adobe bricks handmade by local Indians. Homesteader and carpenter Claude Cooper built the framework and the belfry. The Southern Pacific Railroad Company furnished the bell. The school served as a learning center for children during the day, as a community center for town gatherings and meetings, whenever needed, and a church on Sundays.

However sparse the 1930's accommodations might seem to us today, they were grand by comparison to the conditions endured by turn-of-the-century pioneers. Case in point is this account by George White, the first and only graduate of the new grammar school in Coachella in 1904:

"To get my diploma, it was necessary to take an examination in Banning. Two days before the appointed time, I started out on horseback. The first night I rolled out my blanket under palms at Thousand Palms Oasis. I remember that the coyotes howled mighty close that dark night."

"The second night I slept at the old Whitewater Ranch. The foreman told me that it was a natural stopover for outlaws. I kept one eye peeled all that long night. The next day I took the examination in Banning and started home. I made the trip from Whitewater Ranch to Coachella down the middle of the valley, along the railroad tracks, in one day, a long, long ride, and a lonely one, for a 14-year-old kid."

Earline White Oliver remembers what it was like to be a young African-American girl with Southern roots in the Indio of the 1940s. While she was a fifth-grader at Roosevelt School, hers was one of approximately forty

SCHOOL FACTS

The majority of Indio's public schools are named for U.S. Presidents, including Eisenhower, Hoover, Jackson, Johnson, Madison, Roosevelt, Van Buren, Jefferson and Wilson.

Two newer elementary schools that offer international studies reflect the community's aviation past, and are named after Amelia Earhart and John Glenn.

Above right, President Dwight D. Eisenhower visiting Eisenhower Elementary School in 1962. Jacquie Bethel (right) with daughter Dawn. Photo courtesy of Jacquie Bethel.

Photo courtesy of the Coachella Valley Museum and Cultural Center.

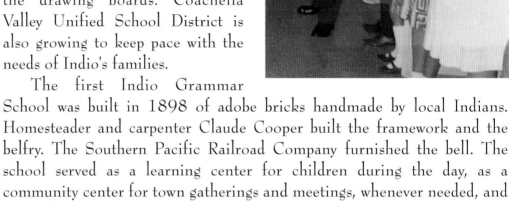

black families to move to the unincorporated area known as Nobles Ranch, where they could raise their own livestock and grow their own vegetables. Her father, Jimmy James White, and her uncle, John Nobles, were leaders in Indio's black community.

As a teenager, Earline rode the bus to Coachella Valley High School with many Japanese and Hispanic students. That experience helped her overcome the sting of segregation, to which her family had been exposed in Texas. Today, as an active older adult, Earline serves on the Desert Sands Unified School District Advisory Board.

Rudy Valenzuela was allowed to skip kindergarten because there was no room for him and he already knew his ABCs. He went straight to Lincoln School and from there to Roosevelt and Jefferson before going off to Coachella Valley High School. His class, 1961, was the last group of Indio kids to graduate from CVHS, since Indio High School was built during that time. "I remember making the Honor Roll in the 7th grade. We got to go on a field trip to Los Angeles. I was from a poor family. We didn't own a car and I had never been outside the valley. That trip was an awakening. I learned there's a big world out there." Rudy has owned and operated Century 21 De Oro Realty since 1982.

Left to right, Cecilia Foulkes, Victoria Bailey, owner of Desert Springs Publishing, and Cecilia's sister Rosalie Johnson.

Above left, Indio High School, circa 1970.

Left, Indio High School Marching Band at Tamale Festival Parade.

Cecilia Foulkes, a revered Mecca School teacher, got her first teaching job at Lincoln School in Indio in 1922. Travel was so strenuous then; Cecilia would stay in Indio and go home to Mecca on weekends, riding the Southern Pacific Sidewinder train for 75 cents. Her students included longtime Indio residents Paul Ames and Frank Cavanaugh. Cecilia Foulkes passed away in July 2004 at the age of 104.

Local author and educator Pat Laflin.

To Your Health

When the railroad came to town, they set up an infirmary to treat workers and keep them productive. About the same time, health sanitariums began springing up across the valley, drawing people from all over the country seeking relief from tuberculosis and respiratory ailments.

One such sufferer was a man by the name of Robinson, who arrived in Indio with his wife, June, a trained physician. It is said that Dr. June intended to spend her days as "a frontier wife," but duty called almost immediately upon her arrival in 1904. She took over as the valley's first resident family physician and supervised a local health camp until it closed in 1908. She continued to serve the local population of railroad and farm families, and, in 1907,

Dr. June Robinson

The first Indio Hospital, operated by Dr. Russell Gray, circa 1930.

was appointed by the Bureau of Indian Affairs to serve as physician to the valley Indian reservations.

Pat Laflin writes in her Coachella Valley California, A Pictorial History, "'Doc June's' territory ranged from Palm Springs to the Salton Sea. There were no real roads to the scattered ranches so she soon abandoned her buggy for a saddle on a spirited horse. Sickness and births came at all hours. Many an operation was performed on the kitchen table, under the glow of a kerosene lamp.

"She said, "'I always carried my instruments with me for it was a long, dusty ride back to the office and there were no telephones. I didn't do major surgery, but I took out lots of tonsils.'"

By 1916, other doctors had arrived. Dr. S. S. M. Jennings intended to farm when he arrived, but also answered the call to serve and became the school district physician, leading a fight against "pink eye," a condition brought about by infestations of eye gnats. An influenza epidemic in 1918 forced Dr. Jennings to order the schools closed. He advised parents with the virus to allow their children to sleep outside in the fresh air. In those days before antibiotics, complications from pneumonia killed one out of every two patients.

In another twist of fate, Dr. Harry Smiley's car broke down in Box Canyon while en route to Los Angeles to set up a practice there. Instead of pushing on, he opened an office in Indio in 1921. His original adobe home on Miles Avenue is the current home of the Coachella Valley Historical Society, Museum and Cultural Center.

Indio's first true hospital was built in 1928 by Dr. Russell Gray. It consisted of three bungalows at the corner of Miles and Towne avenues. Dr. Gray and his wife, a trained nurse, managed the hospital and frequently made house calls to many of 6,000 patients in the area.

From there came Valley Maternity Hospital in Mecca in 1935 and Casita Hospital in Indio, which became Valley Memorial Hospital. Dr. Reynaldo Carreon, a well-known Los Angeles ophthalmologist, proposed a new hospital on land he originally owned on Monroe Street. Indio Community Hosptial was established in 1966 as a community hospital owned by physicians.

> *The new 112-bed Indio Community Hospital on Monroe Street at Avenue 47 will begin operation short after Jan. 1, bringing major new medical facilities to the Coachella Valley. Dr. R. J. Carreon of Indio and Los Angeles, secretary-treasurer of the project, reported that construction of the hospital will be completed Dec. 15, barring strikes or material shortage.*
>
> *Many elaborate and unusual features have been included in the Indio Community Hospital. One feature of the patients' rooms are electric beds. These can be raised to treatment height for bedside care and lowered to dormitory height for patients who are ambulatory. The head and foot controls can be electrically operated by the patient, relieving the nurses of the task of cranking the beds.*
>
> INDIO DAILY NEWS, SEPTEMBER 30, 1965

John F. Kennedy Memorial Hospital

Indio Community Hospital was rededicated as John F. Kennedy Memorial Hospital in 1966. It became a Tenet Healthcare facility in 1979 and serves the community today as a 162-bed, full-service acute care hospital with 24-hour emergency room, surgical services, diagnostic testing and preventive health programs.

JFK Memorial Hospital delivers more than 3,500 babies each year. The Arthritis Institute team has performed over 10,000 total joint replacements. The ER is certified in Pediatric Advanced Life Saving. The hospital continues to be involved in preventive health care programs as well as medical and public health research.

THE EVOLUTION OF HEALTH CARE

1984 - *After securing permission from the Kennedy family, the hospital changes its name to John F. Kennedy Memorial Hospital. Eunice Kennedy Shriver, sister of the late President, attends the dedication ceremony.*
1995 – *NME changes its name to Tenet Healthcare.*
2001 - *JFK establishes a microbiology lab that can perform tests based on scenarios including biochemical attacks and infectious disease outbreaks.*

Eunice Kennedy -Shiver attended the unveiling for the official remaining of John F. Kennedy Memorial Hospital on July 27, 1984.

SHOW AND TELL

In 1977 Bruce Clark bought Abernathy's Union Truck Stop on Highway 99 and the land it was sitting on, mostly to get the coveted Union Oil credit card franchise.

Since he had acquired an amazing collection of porcelain signs depicting country stores and gas stations, he decided to create a miniature travel museum at Clark's Travel Center.

Left to right, Bruce Clark, owner of Clark's Travel Center, John Peters, owner of El Morocco, and Jim Engle, owner of Imperial Signs. All are longtime friends, photo taken January 2005.

Helping Hands

It wasn't all work and no play for Indio's healers. Doctors have always been an important part of the social and civic fabric of the community.

One of the high points of the Indio social season in the 1950s was the annual Coachella Valley Lion's Club show. The sellout fundraiser featured prominent Indio businessmen and leaders dressed in outrageous costumes, singing, dancing, and generally making complete fools of themselves, all in the name of charity.

Dr. Wally Wheeler started practicing medicine in Indio in 1953. He became a member of an active Lion's Club with more than 100 members. One of his volunteer pleasures was writing and choreographing the irreverent Lion's Club comedy skits for nearly a decade, enlisting every fellow physician he could find. Seen here in a 1959 photo are (left to right) Dr. John Shea, Dr. Robert Allison, Dr. Earl Thompson and Dr. Wallace Wheeler, along with Allen Willard and Roger Harlow.

Left to right, Dr. John Shea, Dr. Robert Allison, Dr. Earl Thompson, Dr. Wallace Wheeler, Allen Willard and Roger Harlow at the Coachella Valley Lion's Club annual show, 1959.

Dr. Wally Wheeler was a percussionist before he was a physician, and grew up on big band music. For many years he conducted the Wally "Doc" Wheeler Orchestra, performing at the Riverside County Fair and National Date Festival and other community events. In 2005 he still practices medicine in Indio after 54 years.

The new breed of civic-minded physicians is personified in Dr. Frank Curry. When Dr. Curry is not overseeing the Emergency Room at JFK Memorial Hospital, you might find him presiding over the Indio Chamber of Commerce as President, or serving on the Indian Gaming Commission. Says Curry, "Practicing medicine is rewarding because it helps people and improves our collective quality of life. But I also enjoy my civic involvement because it lets me interact with my friends and neighbors in a more social setting."

Wally "Doc" Wheeler's band.

Getting Around

It didn't take newly mobile Americans long to embrace the car culture once Henry Ford made progress on his pledge to put a Ford in every garage. Dirt roads quickly turned to paved highways as more and more people fed their urge to explore. Smart blacksmiths offered to fix flat automobile tires as well as shoe horses.

The lure of exotic dates and sunny skies drew motorists to the Indio area in the 1930s. Word traveled fast as Indio gained popularity as a tourist attraction.

Coachella Valley Plays Vital Role in Transport Web

The Coachella Valley is a vital transportation hub in Southern California. Since Interstate 10 has been designated as a civil defense route, federal funds have been made available to finance the widening of the freeway from Indio to the west county line. Work is under way to complete the freeway from Indio eastward to the east county line at Blythe.

Southern Pacific Railroad connects the West Coast with such points as New Orleans and Chicago. An average of 45 to 50 trains, most of them freight, pass through Indio daily. Southern Pacific's Indio railroad yard is the largest between Los Angeles and Yuma. [Can't you get on and off the train in Palm Springs to travel by train today?]

Greyhound Bus Line recently completed construction of a large depot in Indio, which probably is the most modern and best-designed bus depot between Los Angeles and Oklahoma City. Nearly all the highways and rail lines in the Coachella Valley converge in Indio; consequently this city is highly geared to transportation services. The city has some 30 service stations and a like number of restaurants

Westward Auto Flow Averages 2 Cars A Minute

Traffic moving westward into California through Blythe, en route to Indio and the Coachella Valley, averages two automobiles per minute. A Riverside County Board of Trade analysis of traffic entering California at Blythe since 1945 showed an average increase of 8.7 percent. "Projecting the average annual increase, by 1983 the traffic entering the state will average 58 automobiles per minute," the Board of Trade said.

INDIO DAILY NEWS, 1965

Needless to say, traffic counts in the 21st Century have skyrocketed beyond anything the early analysts could have imagined. At the moment, Indio is using $29 million in redevelopment bonds to revitalize the downtown area and help it regain its former luster. One of the projects now under way is the realigning of streets leading to the Civic Center, to provide for more of a pedestrian mall around the City Hall complex.

Another downtown project that harkens back to Indio's early days as a transportation hub is a multimodal transportation center proposed for land the city owns on Indio Boulevard. Plans call for the center to have the capability to serve as a passenger terminal for Amtrak train service as well as a "super stop" for local public transit services, taxis and other transportation carriers.

THE SUNKIST TRAIL

Cecelia Foulkes, a beloved Coachella Valley teacher, wrote in her book, "Mecca – A California Desert History," Before Interstate 10 was constructed, Highway 195 on Avenue 66 was the only route to Blythe through Box Canyon. It was then referred to as the "Sunkissed Trail." The route, officially known as The Sunkist Trail, was touted in a newsletter called The Sunkist Trailer as "the shortest and best route between El Paso and Los Angeles - open for travel 365 days a year."

Railroad crossing at Jackson Street and Indio Boulevard before the overpass was built. Photo courtesy of Ben Guitron.

Gimme Land, Lots Of Land

If it weren't for the mighty San Andreas fault, water might not have risen to the desert floor, allowing palm trees to flourish across the Coachella Valley. And, who knows how the real estate market would have developed without the ubiquitous palm to name places after? In the case of "The Walled Oasis of Biskra," elaborate plans for a lush palm-studded paradise never came to fruition.

Above, Landmark North Course, hole #15, "Got Balls?", 183 yards, par 3.

Biskra Palms was a native palm oasis north of Indio where several early Hollywood movies were filmed. In 1928, some enterprising land speculators sold stock in a planned development that was supposed to include a half-million dollar hotel and shops that replicated the ambiance of Casablanca. Employees and merchants were to wear Arabian costumes, and the spires and domes of the oasis would appear like a mirage in the distance as visitors approached.

In 1964, local "Desert Lore" columnist, Paul Wilhelm, recounted the story this way:

The contemplated Oasis of Biskra was no fantasy. Plans had been drawn; thousands of dollars of stock had been sold; 30 colorful tents had been set up under the palms for prospective stock buyers; and sightseeing trips in Hollywood's "Grand Style," had been staged right up until the last, mostly for those flapper stockholders and their movie crowd friends - those who were still under the spell of Rudolph Valentino.

Outdoor Resorts Motorcoach Country Club, (above and right) located on 48th Avenue.

Harry Lawton years ago wrote of that "Jazz Age Dream" as a typical product of the times: "Begun as a sensibly planned project by sensible promoters who became lost in the gaudy extravagance of this heady proposal." The project engineer reported that the Biskra Trust actually raised enough money to build the project, but over-reached its goals in a passion for authenticity. They sent their architect to the Arabian desert to study Saharan architecture, hired a noted Saharan explorer as project manager, and retained the director of the Los Angeles Biltmore to manage the hotel. Then came the bleak news from the marbled halls of Wall Street. The year was 1929 and the stock market crashed.

Despite the setback, time marched on and real estate values

From Wasteland To Bustling Cities: An American Dream Becomes Reality

By John Power, Managing Editor

Amazing. That's the word one would have to use to describe the growth of the Coachella Valley in the last decade. And the end is nowhere in sight. From Palm Springs in the north to Salton City in the south, the sound of construction echoes in an area that once was the home of a few farmers, desert dwellers, prospectors and pioneers.

When did this boom really start and what caused it? Starting in about 1956, developments began taking place in the unincorporated portions of the Valley, mostly in a stretch of desert and date palm country between Palm Springs and Indio.

Expensive country clubs which have attracted such notables as President Dwight D. Eisenhower, the late President John F. Kennedy and Governor Edmund Brown have sprung up. Exclusive homes have been built for such well-known Hollywood stars as Bing Crosby.

At the present time, the Valley has over 18 golf courses with a net worth exceeding $100,000,000. These golf courses have brought a new wealth and a new dimension of desert living. They have sparked a rising wave of economic growth through virtually all parts of the Valley.

Indio Daily News, September 30, 1965

Left to right, Rudy Acosta, Redevelopment/Economic Development Director, Troy Strange, Senior Economic Development Specialist, and former Mayor Jacquie Bethel, at construction site of Starbuck's.

increased. Even in the 1960s, people speculated about how much more the valley could grow.

In a 2004 Indio city profile in *The Desert Sun*, it was reported that more than 50 housing projects are on the drawing boards. They will collectively create some 15,000 dwellings. Projects range in scope from single-family home developments by U.S. Homes, Rilington Communities, Century and Lennar, to condominium and apartment-style projects by S & D and Pacifica, to Pulte Homes' Sun City Shadow Hills' 3,000+ units. Outdoor Resorts is planning 400 recreational vehicle lots.

Lennar Homes' Heritage Palms Golf Club.

On the commercial real estate side, Indio is set to welcome its first Starbucks, a new Cadillac, Chevrolet and Mitsubishi dealership in the I-10 Auto Mall, and a group facilities expansion at the Trendwest Timeshare project within the next two years. In 2003 Indio was the 12th fastest growing city in the state. Experts say if the present growth trend continues, Indio's population will more than double by 2010.

Bountiful Harvests

The U.S. Department of Agriculture Date and Citrus Station put Indio on the map during the infancy of the date farming industry. When scale infestations were discovered on imported date offshoots from the Mediterranean, new offshoots were quarantined for one year. The government quickly sent its best specialist from Phoenix, Arizona, to Indio to supervise the eradication of the scales.

West Coast Turf, founded in 1990, is the West's largest grower and installer of turfgrass sod in 20 different varieties. West Coast Turf has supplied product to the Rose Bowl, Dodger Stadium and Bank One Ballpark in Phoenix as well as golf courses and residential developments all over the world.

Boasting a record any NFL team would envy, West Coast Turf makes its seventh trip to the Super Bowl in 2005, supplying 100,000 square feet of sod for the big game. Sod for the 2004 Super Bowl in San Diego was supplied by West Coast Turf's Indio facility. The turfgrass was harvested and transported a few weeks before game day and installed by the company's trained crew.

The Coachella Valley's crop varieties are diverse and hearty. Today, citrus fruit including oranges, tangerines, grapefruit, lemons and limes are in the top five products exported. But enterprising farmers are also testing and perfecting crops usually associated with other geographic areas, including sweet corn, gourmet herbs, peppers and artichokes.

Table grapes, however, are the Big Daddy of agricultural yield in the east end of the Coachella Valley. Seedless grapes were introduced by early Armenian growers and were later crossbred by viticulturists to improve their taste and texture. The result was the popular Red Flame grape. Today, nearly 15 percent of all California table grapes are grown locally. In 2001, grapes were the second most valuable crop in the Coachella Valley.

Trini Alvarez with oranges just picked at the Valencia orange ranch.

West Coast Turf.

Richard A. Glass Co., Inc., Indio.

Bermuda Dunes
COACHELLA VALLEY
Thompson Seedless Grapes
MINIMUM NET WEIGHT 22 LBS.
PRODUCE OF U.S.A.
Distributed by RICHARD A. GLASS CO., INC., Indio, California

Let's Put On A Show

Today, Indio is known as the City of Festivals. Nearly one million visitors each year visit to enjoy cultural, music, sports, entertainment and culinary events - many of which attract worldwide attention. From Native American Powwows to national girls' field hockey tournaments, there's truly something for everyone.

The Date Festival began as a celebration of the date harvest and was held on and off in various Indio public parks beginning as early as 1921. The first local women to dress in homemade Arabian costumes caused quite a stir in those days. The National Date Festival came into its own in 1938. For a time, the event dropped its Arabian theme and became more of a western celebration and rodeo.

After World War II, the Riverside County Board of Supervisors "drafted" one of their employees, Robert "Bob" Fullenwider, to stage a county fair in Indio. He enlisted the expertise of Stewart Yost, manager of the successful Orange County Fair, and in 1947, brought back the original Arabian theme.

Fullenwider's daughter contributed the additional idea of a beauty contest with the winner being crowned Queen Schcherazade. In that era,

every little town had a crowned Miss who represented her community at pageants throughout the area. The Date Festival had no trouble attracting contestants from miles around. It was typical to have 18 young women housed at the old Hotel Indio with chaperones for 10 days.

Even though the National Date Festival celebrates the annual harvest of a unique agricultural product, not everyone is into the wrinkly brown fruit. Since the event is also the Riverside County Fair, there are plenty of other diversions to amuse fairgoers. Young 4-H Club members bring their livestock to show and auction for sale. Arts, crafts and school-sponsored exhibits display prize-winning handiwork and projects. Ostrich and camel races are crowd-pleasers. Carnival rides and food booths of all varieties are guaranteed to keep everyone in the family entertained. Present day fair attendance typically tops 270,000 people over the 10-day run.

FAIR FACTS

Riverside County purchased the original 40-acre site of the fair in 1940 for $10,000. The Date Festival grounds now comprise 120 acres.

The early Arabian Nights pageant had some heavyweight assistance right from the start. Retired motion picture set designer Harry Oliver conceived and supervised the building of the festival's outdoor stage. Acclaimed New York writer Lousie Dardenelle wrote the first script for the stage play.

Former Festival director Bob Fullenwider hired Robert Maxwell, the winner of the 1932 Olympics high hurdles competition. Maxwell used his media connections and influence to stage early "photo ops," getting press for the Date Festival in popular national magazines such as Life, Esquire and Reader's Digest.

Queen For A Date

The Legend of Queen Scheherazade (Sha-hair-a-zahd), like most ancient fables, is full of blood, lust and greed – with a happy ending. As the story goes, a vengeful king in Baghdad would take a new wife each evening and have her beheaded at dawn. The task of finding a new sacrificial wife each day was turned over to the Grand Vizier, otherwise known as the Chief of Police.

The Chief himself was father to two of the most beautiful maidens in the kingdom – one of whom was Scheherazade. She was known as a comedian and great storyteller. Scheherazade begged her father to take her to the king as a bride. At first he refused, fearing for his daughter's fate. Finally, realizing that her time would eventually come, the Chief relented.

As dawn approached in the king's chamber, Scheherazade began to weave a story of romance, adventure and intrigue so fascinating that the king became spellbound. In true "cliff-hanger" fashion, Scheherazade made sure her story reached an exciting climax just when the king's daily rituals were to begin. He had no choice but to postpone her execution until the following morning if he was to hear the conclusion of the tale. Scheherazade was able to spin her stories for what the pageant celebrates as "One Thousand and One Nights." By that time, according to the legend, the King was in love with Scheherazade and they lived happily ever after.

Tamales Go Big Time

Dave Hernandez, proprietor of the Towne Avenue Barbershop in downtown Indio, was an active member of the Downtown Indio Merchants Association in the early 1990s. The group held breakfast meetings to plan events and marketing strategies to bring people into the downtown area. Other member businesses at the time included Don's Bike Shop, Yellow Mart, CV Furniture, Hotel Indio and the Chamber of Commerce.

Photo of children at lower right courtesy of Mark Bergstrom.

At one of the summer meetings in 1991, Dave Hernandez suggested (and was immediately put in charge of) a tamale festival. A committee was formed with people like Rudy Acosta Sr., Linda Beal, Dick and Russ Friestad, Gilbert Hernandez, Sherry Johnson, Diane Nieto, Jim Preston, Chris Romero, and Chamber of Commerce staff.

The inaugural event was held in December of 1992 called "Feria Internacional de Tamal" and was held at Miles and Smurr Streets. The one-day festival featured 18 tamale vendors, mostly from local apostolic churches, who set up shop with folding tables and brightly colored tablecloths. They sold tamales for $1 apiece. Says Hernandez, "It was very family and community oriented in the early days."

The attendance in 1992 was estimated to be approximately 5,000 people. Since Indio had not held a holiday parade in many years, the Chamber

organized one the following year to tie in with the 1993 festival. The number of vendors grew and the festival gained momentum. It became a two-day event, music and entertainment were added and the name was changed to a more mainstream "Indio International Tamale Festival."

The festival is now referred to by Food Network as one of the Top Ten All-American Food Festivals in the country. It features nearly 80 tamale vendors and 250 purveyors of arts and crafts and holiday items. Food vendors typically sell 300,000 tamales during the two days. Attendance has reached 175,000 people, making it the world's largest tamale festival according to the *Guinness Book of World Records*.

Outstanding In Its Field

The Coachella Valley Music and Arts Festival, more commonly known simply as "Coachella," has, in a few short years, rocketed to the top of the music scene. The Alternative European Rock-style festival is a two-day outdoor event held on the lush green fields of the Empire Polo Club. *Rolling Stone* magazine has called it "The best American rock festival," and England's NME goes a step further to call it "probably the best festival in the world." More than 50,000 fans each day flock to the event from all over the world to enjoy the music, art and short films. The festival, which got its start in 1999, has presented such acts as Beck, Moby, the Red Hot Chili Peppers, Oasis, Weezer, the Pixies and Radiohead.

Top left, left to right, Dick Jandt, Bill Proctor, Dave Hernandez, Mike Savidge, Dick Friestad, Mick Barnhill and son of the owner of Hotel Indio putting the finishing touches on the "world's largest tamale."

Above, volunteer and local legend Chris Romero.

Chef John Sedlar, aka "The Tamale King," author of Modern Southwest Cuisine, is responsible for Indio's 1 foot wide by 40 foot long tamale, which is still a Guinness World Record.

Coachella Valley Music and Arts Festival, 2004.

A Place In History

Historic Mural: History of Water,
near corner of Indio Boulevard and
Fargo Street, artist Don Gray,
completed 2003.

Jacqueline Cochran was appointed to the Women's Air Force Service Pilots (WASP) and received the Distinguished Service Medal.

A Place In History

*I*f the South reveres its women as "steel magnolias," then the desert can certainly take credit for the stamina of its "cactus flowers." The Southern California desert hamlets of the early 1900s might have enticed enterprising men who envisioned lush green fields of profitable harvests. But it was their pioneering womenfolk who endured hardships to make homes, bear children, teach school, care for the sick, encourage the development of culture, and work alongside the men to make the desert bloom.

An active women's club gained prominence in Indio for its community service activities and cultural pursuits. Make no mistake, these ladies were not simply pouring tea and giving sympathy. They were actively working to make their community a better place. And, over the years, they succeeded in making quite an impression well beyond city borders.

When gnats became so persistent and so numerous that they threatened not only the comfort but also the well being of Indio's residents, members of the Indio Women's Club asked researchers at the University of California's Citrus Experiment Station for answers. Mr. J.C. Chamberlin replied to their request, "Curiously enough, in spite of the importance of this pest, little or nothing seems to be known about its status as a disease carrier or means of possible eradication or control."

The Women's Club shot back by "insisting" that a survey be completed immediately. They must have made their point quite effectively. Mr. Chamberlin applied for state aid by saying, "We wish to request that a trained entomologist or other competent man in connection with or under supervision of the State University be detailed to conscientiously and systematically investigate this problem. To that end we are willing, not only to cooperate to the utmost extent, but also, if necessary, to raise a fund to assist in the prosecution of such an investigation."

WOMAN'S CLUB

1912 - *The first women's club - the Altrurian Club - was organized in Indio.*
1914 - *Indio Woman's Club operates a circulating library out of boxes at the Indio Post Office.*
1924 - *Indio Woman's Club moves to its new clubhouse, built for $4,500. It would become one of Indio's best meeting facilities for years to come.*
1944 - *Indio Woman's Club burns the mortgage on its clubhouse, thanks in part to finances buoyed by the lease of the facility to the USO during the war years.*

Woman's Club of Indio, 1924, President was Clara Boyer (3rd from the left). Dr. June McCarroll (in white dress) is standing 8th from the left.

The White Stripe

One of the most dramatic undertakings of the Indio Women's Club took them all the way to the State Legislature.

Dr. June Hill Robertson McCarroll was typical of the true feminine pioneering spirit. She answered the call of duty almost immediately upon arriving when the Indio health camp's resident physician found he could not take the desolation and blowing sand and returned east. Dr. June was not licensed in California but was quickly granted a special permit by the state board of medical examiners.

Dr. June Robertson McCarroll.

Doctor June McCarroll Memorial Freeway

In 2000, State Senator David G. Kelley authored a resolution honoring Dr. June McCarroll by renaming the portion of Interstate 10 between Jefferson Street, Indio Boulevard and Highway 86 for her. A plaque dedicating the tribute was dedicated on April 24, 2002.

Over the course of more than a dozen years, Dr. June traveled dusty, rutted roadways first by horseback and later by automobile to visit patients. Even when dirt roads were paved, sandstorms rendered them dangerous and difficult to navigate. One day, she observed a crease down the center of a newly widened road and came up with the idea of the white stripe. Already retired from her medical practice, Dr. June took up the cause of highway safety.

In 1917, she painted a white stripe down the middle of the road for several blocks in front of her house to showcase her idea. It was said to be the first white centerline in California. Local citizens agreed it was an excellent suggestion. Encouraged, she presented her plan to the Riverside County Board of Supervisors, who listened, thanked her politely and tabled the subject.

Undaunted, she argued her case in front of numerous chambers of commerce and the state highway department. At that point, she remarked, "I came to the belated conclusion that talking to men's organizations had been a waste of time. After five years of persistent effort, I seemed to be getting nowhere. Consequently, I decided to work with the women."

After receiving rousing support from the regional and state federation of Women's Clubs, she carried a resolution petitioning the California State Legislature to enact a law authorizing the State Highway Commission to paint a line down the middle of all state roads. Although she never received official recognition, Dr. June was pleased that subsequent studies confirmed the white centerline decreased the number of highway accidents throughout California.

Road from Indio to Edom, showing the new concept of the center line on roads in the 1920s.

Local Color

Among the legendary figures of early Indio were two Native Americans, whose real-life stories were undoubtedly embellished into more colorful versions with each telling. Ambrosio was a Cahuilla medicine man and "fire eater," who died in 1926 at age 75. Fig Tree John was an Indian scout and larger-than-life personality who was said to have been 136 years old when he died in 1927.

The story of Ambrosio Costillo is intertwined with that of Dr. June Robertson McCarroll. When the Bureau of Indian Affairs appointed Doc June as its first Indian doctor for the five reservations in the Coachella Valley in 1907, tribal medicine men vowed not to give up their calling without a fight.

Ambrosio was already a well-known local performer at fiestas and the earliest Festival of Dates. He was also a Cahuilla medicine man who marveled at the healing that Dr. June brought to Indian patients. He gave up his own healing arts and pledged to work alongside Doc June to carry out her orders. He became her assistant, working night and day through epidemics and enforcing quarantines.

Juanita Razon was supposedly the given name of Fig Tree John. Newspaper accounts say he insisted his parents bestowed the feminine name "Juanita" on him and it was bad luck to change it. Nevertheless, he inherited the nickname Fig Tree John when he planted some of the first fig trees in the valley around the "rancheria" where he lived.

Part of the Fig Tree John legend has him guiding General John Fremont across the mountains into California in the days of the Spanish explorers. He is also said to have kept a secret gold mine in the remote hills. But most controversial was the report of his age - 136 at his death. When asked in 1958 if the stories about his father were true, the legend's aged son, Johnny Mack said, "Maybe so, maybe no."

In his later years, Fig Tree John took to dressing up in a worn-out Army uniform with shiny buttons and a stovepipe hat. He made sure to catch the eye of tourists, for whom he volunteered to pose for a small fee. It is reported he made a handsome living from this sideline. Said one report in the *Press-Enterprise* newspaper, "There is many a place today where he'd be tabbed as just another crackpot. The valley residents never said that about old Fig Tree John. They couldn't. He stood so straight, was so sure of his right to walk free on the land and live as he likes, that he is still remembered as a proud, interesting man."

Left to right in back, Captain Ramon, Captain Jim and Captain Sastro, in front, Captain Habiel, Captain Will Pablo, Chief Cabazon, Captain Manuel and Captain Jose Maria. Photo courtesy of Malki Museum, Morongo Indian Reservation.

Fig Tree John and his wife, circa 1906.

The Sky's The Limit

Any one of Jacqueline Cochran's accomplishments would have made for a full life. The fact that she achieved so many distinctions is a testament to her remarkable spirit. That spirit was celebrated in a big way in 2004 with the renaming of Riverside County's regional airport in Thermal to the Jacqueline Cochran Regional Airport. On opening day, November 6, 2004, the air show "Thunder over the Desert" had over 10,000 in attendance.

Program from opening day of the Jacqueline Cochran Regional Airport, November 6, 2004.

A desert resident for some 40 years, it's no wonder Jackie's personal mantra was, "Reach for the stars." Seeing her considerable success, few can imagine her humble beginnings. She was a foster child raised by a poor family in Florida. She dropped out of school in the third grade and took up the name Cochran legally after finding it in a phone book.

She supported herself by working in a cotton mill and cleaning beauty salons, eventually becoming a licensed cosmetologist and part owner of a hair salon. With the money she earned, she bought a car and drove alone to New York City, landing a job at Saks Fifth Avenue. It wasn't long before she was on her way back to Florida to work in the company's Miami salon.

It was there she met financier Floyd B. Odlum, co-founder of the Atlas

The Pasha of Kenitra, Abdelhamid El Alaoui, presents a gift to President Eisenhower at the Cochran-Oldum Ranch home early in 1962. The Pasha was a cousin of King Hassan II of Morocco At left are Floyd Odlum and wife Jackie.

Corporation, who, at the time, was one of the 10 richest men in the world. They married and embarked on a jet-set life, dividing their time between a Fifth Avenue penthouse in New York City and a sprawling 900-acre ranch in Indio. Odlum encouraged his wife's business endeavors, helping her start her own cosmetics company. He also helped fuel her ambition to learn to fly so that she could travel in her own plane to visit her company stores.

Jackie Cochran

Jackie earned her pilot's license in just three weeks. She competed in and won the Bendix Air Races women's division several times and later conquered the Intercontinental Race, competing against some of the top male pilots of the time. She set distance and altitude records, flying faster than any other woman pilot.

When the U.S. entered World War II, Jackie organized a group of female pilots who helped ferry warplanes back from England. In 1945, after Pearl Harbor, she was appointed to the Women's Air Force Service Pilots, or WASPs, and received the Distinguished Service Medal.

Her service continued as a war correspondent in the Pacific. Cochran was reported to be the first woman to land in Japan after the peace treaty was signed. After the war, she continued her quest for aviation records, all the while running her cosmetics company and overseeing work on the Indio estate. Not only did Jackie select the site for her desert home before she married Floyd Odlum, but she plunged into the construction hands-on, laying bricks, pounding nails, and turning the entire experience into a true do-it-yourself project.

Milestones of Jacqueline Cochran

Set more than 80 aviation records.

In 1941, became the first woman to pilot a bomber across the North Atlantic, flying an RAF aircraft from Canada to England.

In 1953, became the first woman to break the sound barrier in a Sabre Jet F-86. Chuck Yeager was flying off her wing over Edwards Air Force Base when she made the noteworthy accomplishment.

First aviatrix to land on an aircraft carrier.

Retired as a colonel in the Air Force, having logged more than 15,000 flying hours in aircraft of many types.

In 1964, broke her own speed record to reach 1,429 miles per hour, the fastest speed ever attained by a woman pilot.

Went on to unofficially fly 1,900 miles per hour, or Mach 2.5.

First to fly with oxygen masks at ultra high altitudes.

Tested G-suits with experimental massage pads to reduce body stress on pilots.

First woman to test fly with 130 octane gasoline.

Sold her Beechcraft Super E to Merv Griffin in 1972.

United States Postal Service honored Jacqueline Cochran with the issuance of 50-cent international postcard-rated stamp on March 9, 1996.

General Charles (Chuck) Yeager and his wife Glennis were close friends of Jackie and Floyd. Yeager mentored Cochran, helping her achieve her goals.

The In Crowd

The Cochran-Odlum ranch was a sanctuary for heads of state, movie moguls, captains of industry and the super-rich. With its casual atmosphere, private golf course and plenty of room to roam, the ranch afforded dignitaries a place to relax. Even Jackie's good friend, Amelia Earhart, came to the ranch to get away. It is said that she even planned part of her ill-fated flight over the Pacific Ocean while visiting the Indio ranch.

The ranch was also a center of social activity and recreation for Jackie Cochran's many friends in Indio. One of them who still lives in Indio is Bev Hanson Sfingi. Bev's parents were some of the first residents of Indio's Sun Gold area, a popular residential enclave. Bev took up golf at an early age and won the U.S. Amateur in 1950 at the East Lake Country Club in Atlanta. Jackie Cochran and Floyd Odlum sent Bev a congratulatory telegram that she still has to this day.

Bev turned LPGA pro in 1951. During her career, she won 3 major ladies tournaments, including the first one she played in - a feat unmatched in today's LPGA. Bev credits Jackie and Floyd for bringing golf to the eastern Coachella Valley. She remembers that the private O'Donnell course in Palm Springs was considered a "part time" course since its proximity to the mountains causes the sun to go down earlier in the

day. Says Bev, "People started going to Arizona to play golf because the sun shined longer. The Cochran course opened up everybody's eyes to golf in Indio. You could tee off at 1 p.m. and still finish 18 holes." In 1991, a devastating fire ripped through the ranch, doing an estimated $565,000 in damage, believed to be a record money loss for a fire in the Coachella Valley. The *Riverside Press Enterprise* newspaper report said that most of the damage was done in a two-story artist studio and guesthouse where $500,000 worth of original oil paintings and antiques were lost.

The Desert Sun and the Los Angeles Times reported on the November 6, 2004 re-dedication of the Desert Resorts Regional Airport in Thermal as the Jacqueline Cochran Regional Airport. The event was marked with one of the largest air shows ever held in Riverside County, with a full day of events and crowds estimated at more than 35,000. The airport, which serves executive and corporate jets, was recently outfitted with $20 million in improvements.

The former Cochran-Odlum Ranch is now the site of Indian Palms Country Club. The gated community features 27 holes of championship golf with a full clubhouse, golf shop, fitness center, restaurant and bar. The property also boasts a 59-room boutique hotel. First Pacific Development Corporation offers six different residential housing enclaves within Indian Palms' gates.

Right, General Henry H. "Hap" Arnold presented one of the several Harmon Trophies won by Jacqueline Cochran. General Arnold had been taught to fly by Wilbur and Orville Wright in 1911.

In The Limelight

Indio continued to be the center of newsworthy events. Some made it to the public's attention while some events were seen simply as daily occurrences that have since been passed along by personal recounting.

The local date growers association was vigilant in alerting the country to the Coachella Valley's bounty. Point-of-purchase displays were set up in supermarkets across the country, touting the taste and versatility of cooking with dates. This newspaper article chronicles the effort.

The year 2006 marks the 60th anniversary of the Riverside County Fair & National Date Festival. To help celebrate the occasion, fair officials are calling for all former scholarship winners who were selected as Queen Scheherazade, Princess Jasmine or Princess Dunyazade to assemble together in Indio for another round of applause.

An *Indio Daily News* item from the mid 1960s made this observation:

Date Campaign In Full Swing

Millions of American housewives will become keenly aware during the next few months that only the plump, delicious Coachella Valley dates really carry that irresistible taste of sunshine. At least that is the goal of the marketing division of the California Date Growers Association.

By radio, newspapers and through market displays, the entrancing story of California dates - the "candy that grows on trees" - will be told during the months ahead as the more than 30 million pounds of fruit comes off the packing line in the Cal Date plant here.

Much of the fruit is being packed in special brand packages for many of the food and market giants of the country - Safeway, Pillsbury, Calavo and many more. Much store is being put into the tremendous radio promotion that started in the middle of September on the nationwide radio circuit where Dan McNeil and Arthur Godfrey, two of the principal "salesmen" of the airwaves, held forth.

The two stars, heard daily by about 12 million listeners over 552 stations of the ABC and CBS systems, boost the dates four days a week. Their enthusiastic endorsement of the fruit, together with suggestions for its use, is beamed to all corners of the U.S.

INDIO DAILY NEWS - SEPTEMBER 30, 1965

A Daily News *columnist got into a tiff with a producer of the TV game show Jeopardy in the late 1960s when the show's host stated that Palm Springs was the Date Capital of the U.S. Phil Ault, author of the "Desert Cavalcade" column stuck with his rant until the TV show was forced to admit its sources were incorrect.*

Newspapers in 1970 reported that June 26 was the hottest day in 60 years. Imperial Irrigation District general manager Ray Rinderhagen stated that the daytime high of 123 degrees in Indio and 126 in Thousand Palms was the highest temperature noted since record-keeping started in 1947.

Not So Trivial Pursuits

Prior to the opening of its Special Events Center, Fantasy Springs has hosted a number of large-scale events that have attracted national and international attention. In 2003 and 2004, the casino hosted contestant tryouts for TV's "Wheel of Fortune" and "Jeopardy" games shows, both of which were created by part-time desert resident Merv Griffin.

Nearly 5,000 people turned out for both tryouts, where staffers from the TV shows interacted with participants and randomly selected potential contestants to be considered for future appearances on the nationally-televised programs.

From 1995 to 2001, Fantasy Springs was the site of 30 World Championship boxing events featuring names like "Sugar" Shane Mosley, Bernard Hopkins, Eric "Butterbean" Esch and Henry Akinwande. Boxer Antonio Diaz appeared many times and was a crowd favorite, being a product of the Coachella Boxing Club. The matches were not just audience pleasers, they were celebrity magnets. Among the famous faces in the crowd were Bruce Willis, Mr. T, "Magic" Johnson, Steve Garvey, Tony Dorsett and Oscar De La Hoya. The boxing match-ups were delivered to a national audience on Showtime, HBO, ESPN and Fox Sports channels.

Black History Month

For more than a decade, the Coachella Valley Museum and Cultural Center housed stacks of archives detailing the history of Native Americans, white settlers and Hispanic pioneers, but had little information on the contributions of African-Americans. That situation began to change in the late 1990s with a cultural celebration during

"Sugar" Shane Mosley at Fantasy Springs. Photo courtesy of Johnny R. Gonzalez.

Black History Month. Early black residents contributed photos and artifacts to a museum display and invited the community to join them in hearing from keynote speakers like Bishop C.E. Simmons of Mount Calvary Holy Church.

A 1958 story in *The Coachella Valley Sun* newspaper details the development of Nairobi Desert Estates, a subdivision of 89 homes on 20 acres. Photos accompanying the story depicted early Nairobi

Former mayor and city councilman Marcos Lopez with guest attending Black History Month at the Coachella Valley Museum and Cultural Center.

homeowners including Mr. and Mrs. Herbert King, Mrs. R. Gene Wilson, and the Fred Weathertons. The story describes the homes as "three bedroom homes of pumice block that are attractively planned, with a choice of four basic plans."

That was a far cry from the experience of the first black settlers like Ola Mae Howard who arrived in 1939 to find a dusty, hot desert outpost where "the insect plagues were like something out of the Bible." Another resident,

Cora Bell Johnson, who helped organize the Black History events, said the history was important because the pioneers had so many obstacles to overcome. "I think it's good for the young people to know. Many of them take for granted the things we have today," Mrs. Johnson observed.

During the war years in the 1940s, segregation was still common. A United Service Organization (USO) for whites was set up at the Indio Elks Lodge while black servicemen frequented a second club on Requa Street. During the same time, Indio had two cafes catering to black clientele.

Left to right, local residents Ward Grant, Mrs. Melvina McDowell and Mitchell McDowell.

Susie Whitman-Maddox came to Indio in 1931. She worked for the Pawley family and Judge Kirby Hester. She was also an entrepreneur who owned several businesses in Indio including a laundry and a restaurant called The Susie Q Café.

John Nobles came to Indio in the 1930s. He bought land and became the first black sharecropper. Piece by piece, Nobles sold the property to black workers so they could build homes of their own. There was a period when the Nobles Ranch residents fought with the city over the availability of water and electricity. In 1990, 87 homes, a public housing project and three churches in the Nobles Ranch area were razed by the city under the provisions of eminent domain to make way for an expansion of the Indio Fashion Mall. For various economic reasons, the mall expansion was put on hold and the fallout at the time was lawsuits and hard feelings.

Louis Strange moved to Indio in 1960 and became the first black professional house painter, belonging to Local #1627. He established Strange Painting and Construction in 1978 and got his contractor's license. His five sons helped him in the business, which included on its client list Groucho Marx, Bob Hope and Red Skelton.

The Mexican-American Vision

One individual who worked tirelessly for more than 50 years for the betterment of his people and his community was Dr. Reynaldo J. Carreon, Jr. Even as a young boy, Dr. Carreon's Mexican father encouraged him to become bilingual and commit himself to the principles of initiative, vision and determination.

The young Reynaldo made his was to Los Angeles where he pursued his medical studies, becoming a noted ophthalmologist and M.D. In the 1950s, he was chosen by President Eisenhower to represent the United States as Ambassador at Large to Central and South America. He also pursued a number of charitable and civic endeavors in keeping with his goal to instill leadership in Mexican youth.

Dr. Reynaldo J. Carreon, Jr. Academy, kindergarden through 5th grade.

Dr. Carreon was a co-founder of Indio Community Hospital (now JFK Memorial Hospital) and donated land for public parks and access to wells for Indio's underground water supply. The street running between the hospital and his original ranch site was renamed in his honor in 1984.

At left, Dr. Carreon, Jr. and wife Lucille.

Dr. Carreon, Jr. and President Richard M. Nixon. Photo courtesy Lucille Carreon and Cal State University, San Bernardino.

Though Dr. Carreon passed away at the age of 91 in 1991, his legacy lives on in the Reynaldo J. Carreon M.D. Foundation, the motto for which is "Creating a Fountain of Knowledge through Leadership, Education & Community Involvement." The foundation has provided more than $250,000 in scholarship funds to more than 400 Mexican American students.

His legacy of learning was also passed on to his children. Daughter Manon went on to become an optometrist in the Los Angeles area while son Rudy became a chemist. Dr. Carreon's wife, Lucille, has remained in Indio until this day and gets great satisfaction out of the good work her husband's foundation continues to do for the Mexican youth of the Coachella Valley.

Desert Sands Unified School District also honored Dr. Carreon with the naming of the Dr. Carreon Academy, one of six magnet schools that specialize in specific career programs and opportunities. The academy offers programs with a health and science focus. Fittingly, the school is located on Monroe Street across from JFK Memorial Hospital.

Dr. Carreon and friends at the Date Festival. Photo courtesy of Paul Ames.

Another of Dr. Carreon's suggestions that took hold was the creation of the Coachella Valley Mexican American Chamber of Commerce, or CV-MACC. Carreon had been involved in a similar organization in Los Angeles, and believed that Hispanic business owners throughout the Coachella Valley could benefit from sharing resources and expertise.

Martin Martinez, the current Executive Director of the Carreon Foundation, remembers a group coming together to explore the idea and meeting with the California Hispanic Chamber of Commerce. Some people wanted the local organization to be a Hispanic Chamber, others insisted on the Mexican-American focus, since that was the true heritage of most of the potential members. CV-MACC was launched with great success and has picked up momentum from the start.

By the time Pamper Rodriguez came to the valley in 1989, her sister had already run Al's Family Shoe Store in downtown Indio for many years, and her nephew, Art Torres, was involved as one of the founders of CV-MACC. Pamper immediately joined the Jaycees to become involved in community activities. In her professional life, Pamper worked her way up the ranks of various Hispanic media organizations around the valley.

Rudy Acosta, Sr. and his wife Ester in their store, Acosta's Furniture, circa 1956.

Rodriguez is currently General Manager of *El Informador del Valle*, a Spanish-language newspaper that focuses on the community and provides an alternative voice not just for Hispanics but for local employers and businesses that need to reach the substantial Spanish speaking market. In 2005, Pamper becomes the first Latina chair of the Indio Chamber of Commerce.

She has remained active with CV-MACC as well, and was designated as Director of the Year in 1998. About CV-MACC, Rodriguez says, "The name says it all. Our mission is to help businesses all over the valley and empower our youth with ongoing education and scholarships."

The Acosta Family is another Indio success story. Rudy Acosta, Sr., who picked carrots as a teenager, became a salesman for Valley Furniture and, eventually, opened his own store, Acosta's Furniture, on Indio Boulevard in 1956. He and wife Esther took advantage of the redevelopment boom in the 1970s to open Coachella Valley Furniture on Fargo Street in 1973.

Chamber of Commerce ribbon cutting at Coachella Valley Furniture on Fargo Street, 1973.

Acosta was known for being especially loyal to the Hispanic community, extending credit to families who couldn't get it elsewhere. He was also active in many civic organizations and became the first Hispanic president of the Indio Chamber of Commerce. Even after Rudy's death, Esther stayed in Indio to retire. Son, Rudy Jr., is currently the City of Indio's Director of Economic and Redevelopment.

Catching the Vision

Historic Mural: History of the Date Industry in the Coachella Valley, artist Chuck Caplinger, completed 1998.

The City of Indio enters an era of unprecedented growth.

Catching the Vision

I ndio is a community with a rich history that has withstood the test of time. As its population swells, Indio is building on its traditions of community service and pride. Public safety, cultural enrichment and civic involvement are some of the "human assets" Indio holds dear.

"Catch the Vision" is the slogan used to market Indio's mature community benefits as well as its innovative and youthful outlook for the future. The catch phrase and logo were designed to give a sense of preserving the past and propelling the community into an even brighter future for residents and visitors alike.

A "Catch the Vision" section of the City's website outlines the many components that contribute to Indio's long-range plan for success. The City's Economic Development Agency has identified four commercial/retail corridors that will allow for optimum growth in Indio's current and future business base.

Each location was chosen based on its unique location to attract and retain high impact businesses. Area 1 is the Highway 111 Hospitality Corridor Gateway. This is an area of 200 acres of lots ranging from 3 to 20 acres in size, zoned for mixed use. Area 2 is the Indio Fashion Mall. Plans are under way to renovate and expand the existing structures into a combination of lifestyle center and traditional shopping complex.

Area 3 is the downtown triangle that was the original city center. The area consists of approximately 588 parcels, 83% of which are improved, occupying 112 acres. Revitalization plans calls for a unique urban experience combining mixed-use retail, office, live-work space, and high density residential and open space for pedestrian activities. Area 4 is the Interstate 10 Freeway Corridor. Indio has four interchanges along 1-10 that provide excellent opportunities for travel, lodging, dining and related services.

Proposed amphitheater and plaza viewed from Civic Center Drive.

EXPLOSIVE GROWTH
Population Trend: 49,116 in 2000, 131,000 in 2010, 208,739 in 2020 Total Permit Valuation: $112 million in 2001 $171 million in 2002 $268 million in 2003

IDEAL LOCATION
On the NAFTA Highway, offering a direct link to Mexico.

AFFORDABILITY
Low utility rates for water and power.

ADDED BENEFITS AND INCENTIVES
Enterprise Zone state tax credits. Empowerment Zone federal tax credits. City redevelopment project area offers assistance.

WEBSITES
City of Indio's website: www.indio.org City of Indio's Catch the Vision website: www.catchthevision.com

In 1958, the Indio Police Department, 16 staff members strong, moved to a new building on Towne Street, which is the present location of the Indio Senior Center.

Top right, Police Cadets, left to right, Scott Rice, Daniel Bojorquez, Jimmy Placentia, Doug Haynes, Sylvia Garcia, and Ben Guitron, 1955. Photo courtesy of Kiki Haynes.

JUST THE FACTS

Law and order came to Indio in the early 1900s when John Boatwright became Constable for the Justice Court and began to administer his brand of frontier justice. The first jail, built in 1920 from railroad ties standing on end, was only eight feet square. When Indio incorporated in 1930, Boatwright filled in as Chief of Police before Francis A. Koehler assumed the role.

Keeping The Peace

In 1932, the entire police department consisted of the chief and three officers. They shared a small office in the first City Hall, which did double-duty as the courthouse. Buela Nyback was Francis Koehler's stepdaughter. She remembers a story about her father jumping onto the running board of a bootlegger's car to arrest him.

In the 1940s, a separate wing was added, complete with a small 12-bunk jail. The department had one patrol car, but it had no radio. When an officer was needed, a bright light mounted atop City Hall was switched on.

Retired Officer Darwin Oakley began walking Indio's beat in 1955 where the work week was nine hours a day, six days a week and the job paid "top money" at $279 a month. The town was so small, Oakley knew most residents by name, where they lived and the names of all their children. In addition to handling major crimes of the time - burglaries and bad checks, officers not only had to patrol the 593 downtown parking meters but clean and oil the meters as well.

In 1962, the department added female meter maids to the force and in 1964 the first woman police officer received her badge. In 1979, the department relocated to its new $1.1 million Jackson Street complex. By 1980, the Indio PD swelled to 75 men and women, including 53 sworn peace officers.

As one of the Coachella Valley's rapidly growing communities, Indio and its Police Department are bracing for the addition of 24,000 homes by the end of 2005. The department's current 62 peace officers will double within the next 10 years thanks to the developer-paid Capital and Public Safety Impact Fee.

"With safety as the core of our goal, Indio Police Department's motto is 'Our Community, Our Commitment,'" boasts Public Information Officer Ben Guitron, who started with the police as a cadet at age 13. "Almost 90 percent of our employees, including Police Chief Brad Ramos, live in Indio. It is the department's plan to meet the city's expectation of having the safest, most balanced, and economically sound community in the valley."

Supporting The Peacekeepers

An important part of Indio's "Catch the Vision" philosophy is bringing a high-profile, a state-of-the art police facility to downtown Indio.

In the mid-1990s, the Police Department took a proactive role in bringing law enforcement and the community together. The Police Cadet Explorers program fosters youth interest in law enforcement as a career and has produced many of Indio PD's officers. One example is 24-year-old Daniel Bojorquez, who was active in the program while attending Indio High School.

After graduation from College of the Desert's Police Science Academy, he was hired as a Code Enforcement Dispatcher and went on to become a sworn peace officer. "Being in the police cadets program helped me reach my ultimate goal," said Bojorquez. "The leadership and moral teaching structure really confirmed my idea of wanting to become a cop."

Citizens Helping Indio Police (CHIPs), left to right, Ben Guitron, Joseph Cornelison, Jerry Barba, Doris Hunt, Med Jeansonne, Alex Levine and Craig Ramsey, 1996. Photo courtesy of Kiki Haynes.

Citizens Helping Indio Police (CHIPs) is a corp of volunteers over 18 years old who patrol high visibility and residential areas. CHIPs members provide up to 900 hours per month, performing traffic control, writing parking or littering tickets, and assisting in code enforcement. Former Nobles Ranch pioneer Earline Oliver is 80 years old and has been in CHIPs for almost nine years. She still drives a patrol car every Friday.

Thanks to local residents who donate the use of personal aircraft, Indio Police Department has an Air Support Division to aid with traffic congestion or extradition of prisoners.

Indio's Police Chiefs

Francis A. Koehler	1930-1932
Leonard "Cy" Sanford	1932-1935
David J. McFerran	1936-1939
Lee O. Smith	1939-1942
P. H. Cunningham	1942-1943
Paul Ackley	1943-1944
P. H. Cunningham	1944
James H. Jones	1945-1946
Charles P. Blake	1946
P. H. Cunningham	1946-1961
Homer L. Hunt	1961-1979
Curtis R. Cross	1980-1985
Jerry N. Graves	1986-1992
Ray "Tom" Ramirez	1992-1998
George E. Rawson	1998-2001
Bradley S. Ramos	2002
	to Present

It is customary in law enforcement circles to design commemorative badges to celebrate significant milestones. So it was that the staff of the Indio Police Department collaborated to create a police shield to mark the establishment of the department on August 18, 1930. The badge will be available to be worn by sworn peace officers and personnel until January of 2006.

Another innovative program is the Indio Youth Task Force, whose mission is to foster extensive networking with several county agencies, youth organizations and service providers for the purpose of juvenile intervention and education.

Fighting Fires

Fire destroyed several downtown Indio businesses on July 4, 1930, less than two months after the city's incorporation. The George Lewis building on Fargo Street was completely lost, claiming a billiard parlor, jewelry store and mercantile. The Indio Fire Department and a crew from Southern Pacific were able to save adjoining buildings while members of the Coachella Fire Department rescued the First National Bank building from danger.

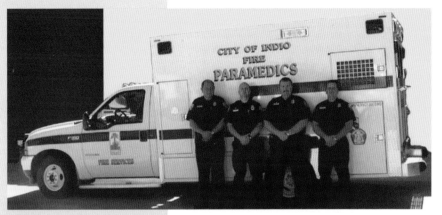

In 1932, the wait for a new fire engine ended with the procurement of a rig described in *The Date Palm* newspaper as a Seagraves with 90-horse power engine. The news account went on to say "The board has ruled that when the 'little engine' is called to the country, a charge of $10 will be made for the engine and a donation to the firemen's fund of $25 is expected. This arrangement is expected to relieve an awkward situation. Whenever a fire occurs in the country, there is always a hurry-up call for the Indio department."

Fire Paramedics left to right, FAE/Paramedic Warren Mueller, FF/Paramedic Jeff Stout, FF/Paramedic Kyle Smith and FF/Paramedic Robert Beeson.

In 1934 arrangements were made between Riverside County and the Indio Fire District to build a new fire station. The County furnished all the labor while the fire district contributed the land and materials. That same year, the Indio Fire Department was named "the best volunteer fire department in the state" by the Board of Fire Underwriters.

In 1945 when World War II was officially declared over on August 16, V J Day (Victory over Japan) was celebrated. Volunteer Fire Chief Harry McCausland blew his whistle every few minutes throughout the night and into the next morning to signal the celebration. In 1948 fire threatened to consume an entire business block on Jackson Street near Tingman. Among the damaged businesses were Carmody's Newsstand, Cavanaugh Electric and Western Auto Supply.

Harry McCausland was also know as "Mr. Fireman," and served as chief of the Indio Volunteer Fire Department until 1956 when the city hired its first full-time paid fire chief. Bruce Clark acquired the brass bell given to Harry McCausland on his retirement. It is on display at Clark's Travel Center.

In 1949 fire destroyed the Assembly of God Church at Requa and Second Street. The loss was estimated at $60,000, including $4,000 in instruments owned by the 20-piece church orchestra. The building was not covered by insurance, a $16,000 policy having lapsed two months earlier. In 1950 fire swept through three floors of Hotel Indio after soot and cooking grease in vents over the cooking range and ovens ignited. Damage was confined to four rooms, the kitchen and basement.

Today's Indio Fire Department is made up of one Division Chief, two Battalion Chiefs, one Fire Marshal, two Fire Safety Specialists, one Fire Inspector, 35 paid Firefighters, 22 Volunteer Firefighters, one Office Assistant, and three fire Explorers. The team uses a variety of equipment designed to answer all types of emergencies, including one Telesquirt Engine, two Front Line Engines, one Reserve Engine, two Front Line Medic

Units, two Reserve Medic Units, one Water Tender and eight Support Vehicles.

The department stands at the ready to respond to more than 4,200 calls per year, or 350 per month, ranging from fire suppression to emergency medical, to public service response to fire menace standbys. Year 2005 will see the addition of another Medic Engine and a 100 foot aerial ladder truck. Station #4 is expected to come on line in 2006 at Avenue 40 & Madison Street. The cost for 12 truck firefighters and operations will be shared by the adjoining jurisdictions that will share the service response. By 2009-2010, City Fire will operate five engine companies, one ladder truck, and four paramedic ambulances.

Indio firefighters have at their disposal two thermal imaging cameras to locate civilians or firefighters trapped in smoky-fire

Hotel Indio burns to the ground, December, 2004. Photo courtesy of Johnson's Photo.

conditions or fire smoldering in walls and other concealed areas. Coming soon are laptop computers with GPS technology to assist dispatching. The computers could serve as mobile command centers with street mapping, fire hydrant locations, floor plans and type of construction of commercial, and hazardous chemical storage data.

Indio Fire Chiefs

1925–1932	*Web C. Kelley*
1932–1956	*Harry "Mac" McCausland*
1956-1959	*Ray G. Roberts (First paid, full time Fire Department Chief)*
1959-1966	*Cy Adams*
1966-1971	*Robert Fink*
1971-1972	*Marcel Beauchamp & Mark Markovich*
1972-1980	*H.W. Denne*
1980-1990	*John F. Payne*
1990-1991	*Richard Ligman*
1991-1996	*Ken Hammond*
1996-1997	*Robert A. Green & Dorian Cooley*
1997-2003	*Dorian Cooley & Tom Foley*
2003-Present	*Dennis Dawson*

1960 *An arsonist destroyed three major Indio businesses within five days. The Aladdin Theater on Miles Avenue, Valley Lumber, and Valley Date on Indio Blvd. burned.*

1966 *The two-story Southern Pacific depot, considered the oldest building in the Coachella and Imperial valleys, burned to the ground.*

1984 *The city's most spectacular fire occurred on October 25, 1984, destroying one of the city's largest employers, the Cal Date Company plant on Indio Blvd.*

1991 *Fire leveled the Hotel Potter and two adjoining commercial buildings. High winds blew embers across Jackson Street overpass and ignited two dozen palm trees. A nine-hour fire fight with numerous mutual-aid fire units from throughout the Coachella Valley prevented the blaze from burning the entire block of Fargo Street.*

Business Boosters

The Indio Chamber of Commerce has worked hand in hand with city government, utility and service providers, educators, public safety and law enforcement officials and community business leaders to keep Indio's economic engine firing on all cylinders. Throughout the years, Chamber directors have

Proposed Chamber of Commerce and Plaza, view from Indio Boulevard.

served on the City Council and vice versa, creating a strong and vital partnership for Indio's citizens and businesses.

The Chamber serves as the visitors' center, providing information and promoting tourism. It also serves as the city's special event facilitator, supplying volunteers and marketing assistance for the variety of events held

Indio Chamber CEO Sherry Johnson

year-round in the city that calls itself the "City of Festivals." On the economic development front, the Chamber provides statistics and demographic information to potential new businesses and entrepreneurs.

In 1955, Indio celebrated its 25th year of incorporation with a special edition of *The Date Palm* newspaper. The Chamber of Commerce took out a full-page ad inviting residents to a community celebration in the city park.

The message in the ad read:

Some cities are hundreds of years old…some cities are thousands. Compared to them, Indio is brand-new. Some cities are growing fast…some not so fast. But, compared to Indio, most of them are just standing still. Yet, the real measure of a city is not its age or its rate of growth, but its people. And, we the people of Indio, have a rare opportunity…a brand-new city with a high destiny to do with what we will.

Indio was born 25 years ago as just another village in the Coachella Valley. Now, a quarter of a century later, our Anniversary is a day of new birth into a new role. We are living a fairy tale of a Cinderella city…born a very ordinary village…but destined to be, as if by magic…the Queen City of the Desert.

The Chamber is in the process of moving to a new downtown location that will become an anchor for the revitalization efforts there. Says Indio Chamber CEO Sherry Johnson, "We're excited that the Indio Chamber is going back to its roots in our historic downtown where the city got its start."

Beauty And The Beasts

Indio is also known as the Polo Capital of the West. When you combine the land area of two of America's finest polo facilities - Eldorado Polo Club and Empire Polo Club - you have the world's largest facility of its kind with 12 tournament polo fields and stabling for more than 1,000 horses.

Polo is known as the "sport of kings," and has been played for centuries the world over. Owner Alex Jacoy reports that Eldorado Polo Club dates

back more than 50 years, and has hosted virtually every major U.S. tournament as well as its share of celebrities and royalty. The club has become a favorite setting for upscale social events within its 185 acres because of its clubhouse and cantina.

Alex Haagen III opened Empire Polo Club in 1987. The venue made polo history when it hosted the first 40-goal tournament played in the United States. Since then, the site has grown into a multi-use venue for concerts, corporate and special events, rodeos and other sporting events. Within this 175 acre site there are beautiful areas for weddings, meetings and picture taking such as the rose garden with its beautiful gazebos and bronze statues.

Since 1992, Horse Shows In The Sun, Inc. (HITS) has produced the largest hunter/jumper horse show west of the Mississippi, the annual Indio Desert Circuit at HITS Desert Horse Park. According to Sport Management Research Institute of Florida, the total economic impact of the six-week Indio Desert Circuit horse show on the surrounding communities exceeds $121 million per year.

John Eickman, HITS National Marketing Director, emphasizes that the event attracts nearly 11,000 horsemen with 3,500 horses. Horsemen compete in 300 different classes in 10 competition rings for $1 million in prize money. Says Eickman, "Our participants represent one of the richest demographics of any sports market."

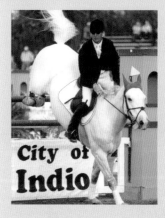

City of Indio

CITY OF FESTIVALS

January - March
Indio Desert Circuit Horse Show, www.hitsshows.com
January - February
Southwest Arts Festival www.southwestartsfest.com
February
Riverside County Fair & National Date Festival www.datefest.org
March and October
Indio Powwow www.cabazonindians.com
April
Salsa Festival www.salsafest.org
May
Coachella Valley Music & Arts Festival www.coachella.com
July
Fourth of July Festival www.indio.org/festivals.htm
December
International Tamale Festival www.tamalefestival.org

CREATING A MUSEUM

It was on The Smiley's property that the first date fair with Arabian-theme costumes was held.

The thick adobe walls of the Smiley house were built from bricks made from local soil by local artisan, Juan Rivera, who also worked on the La Quinta Hotel. Steel railroad rails were used inside the walls.

The house was designed for year-round living. Each room had an electrical outlet to plug in a fan. The cool basement was planned as a warm weather escape. The garage roof was constructed to double as a sleeping porch.

At top right, Coachella Valley Museum and Cultural Center. At middle right, Dr. Harry Smiley. At bottom right, Coachella Valley Pioneers Association, circa 1950.

Preserving A Legacy

The existence of a Pioneers Society in Indio dates back to the 1920s. Dr. June Robertson McCarroll, Elizabeth Moore, and Mr. and Mrs. Francis Koehler are among the townspeople shown below in a 1930s photo taken at a picnic in what was known as the railroad clubhouse park, near the Southern Pacific depot, where many community events took place.

In 1963, the Coachella Valley Pioneers' Association circulated a

petition in support of creating a museum in Indio. To give their idea more momentum, the Coachella Valley Historical Society was formed in 1964 with Otho Moore, son of original pioneer Elizabeth Moore, as president.

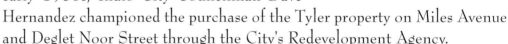

Over the next 20 years, Indio residents and family members donated items of interest relating to Indio's history. In the early 1980s, Indio City Councilman Dave Hernandez championed the purchase of the Tyler property on Miles Avenue and Deglet Noor Street through the City's Redevelopment Agency.

He believed the former Dr. Smiley residence, one of the few remaining adobe structures in the valley, was perfectly situated in an area of downtown Indio that was worth preserving and revitalizing. The adobe home was built in 1926 and, at the time, was the most elaborate house in town. It encompassed 3,500 square feet that housed Dr. Smiley's medical practice, living quarters and a maid's room. An additional 1,100-square-foot basement was opened up to house the wives of soldiers stationed at Camp Young during World War II.

With renovations complete and the interior stocked with memorabilia, the Coachella Valley Museum and Cultural Center opened to the public in 1984. Displays include local Indian artifacts, the story of the formation of the Salton Sea, the history of water resources and the development of agriculture in the desert (with emphasis on the date industry). Collections include pioneer family keepsakes, railroad souvenirs, a complete 1926 kitchen and period machinery used by farmers and blacksmiths.

By 1991, the museum was incorporated and gained the "California Point of Historical Interest" designation by the Riverside County Historical Preservation Commission. The extensive landscaped grounds have been rented for weddings and other special events.

The 1909 schoolhouse was renovated in 2004. It is open to the public adjacent to the Coachella Valley Museum and Cultural Center.

Three individual gardens are planted in different themes - a rose garden, a Japanese garden and a desert garden. According to current President Doug York, "Very few communities in Riverside County have a museum of this caliber."

The helping hands of local volunteers have nurtured the museum to its 20th anniversary in 2004. Plans are under way to hire professional staff to manage the expanding archives and exhibits. Included in the Historical Society's master plan for future development is the use of a recently renovated 1909 schoolhouse as a children's programming center. A freestanding building dedicated to the history of the date is set to include an active date grove and packing display. The former Indio Library at Miles Park is planned to hold large art shows and expand youth arts programs. A former apartment building will be transformed into an archive and collection center.

At left, the Society's latest Museum Angel award was given by Cherry Ishimatsu to Walt Geisler and Peg Muir at the Annual Railroad Dinner, May 2004.

"As the second generation of Geissler's to make an earnest living in agriculture, I'm honored to toil a bit longer, to assist the museum preserve the last 100 years of the date industry. The living date garden will feature 12 to 20 trees, and the new museum will tell the date culture story through artifacts, antiquities, farming equipment, books and photographs," said museum volunteer Walt Geisler.

American Pride

The 3,000-square-foot Cabazon Cultural Museum on the grounds of Fantasy Springs Resort Hotel and Special Events Center presents the past, present and future of the Cabazon Band of the ancient Cahuilla culture.

On display are objects that illustrate the historical perspective of the Cahuilla Indians such as utensils and implements used for hunting, fishing, gathering, farming, manufacturing and housekeeping. Hands-on interactive exhibits are designed for children and adults to learn from and enjoy.

The museum also has modern relevance, with exhibits focusing on the contemporary history of the Cabazon Band of Mission Indians. Future plans call for the museum to grow to 10,000 square feet with the construction of a new Tribal Administration facility.

When Joseph and Ruth Chiriaco took up residence at Shavers Summit in 1933, it was a true desert outpost. In the 1950s, a Post Office was established in the community and officials gave Joseph the option of changing the locale's name to Chiriaco Summit in recognition of all the work he'd put into preserving the history of the former Camp Young, headquarters for General George Patton.

Margit Chiriaco Rusche remembers her parents' dedication to the men who served under Patton at the Desert Training Center nearby. By 1985, the Bureau of Land Management had been charged with protecting the 18,000 square miles that once encompassed Patton's remote training operation. They erected a monument at Chiriaco Summit and suggested that Margit head up an effort to create a museum.

The Chiriaco Family donated 7 acres of land on Interstate 10, and a project committee set out to acquire artifacts for the collection. The undertaking got off to a stellar start with President Gerald Ford as the inaugural honorary chairperson and Mrs. Omar Bradley as the second. Fundraising took off. The group even received $1,000 from Bob Hope.

The General Patton Memorial Museum opened in 1988 in a converted Department of Motor Vehicles office that was trucked in from Coachella. Exhibits display memorabilia from the life and career of General Patton, depictions of military life and information on Southern California's water development and the building of the Colorado Aqueduct.

On Veteran's Day 2005, State Senator Jim Battin and Congresswoman Mary Bono are expected to help the museum commemorate the 30th anniversary of the Vietnam War and honor the people who fought in it with a special program of events open to the public.

WILD BIRD CENTER

The Coachella Valley Wild Bird Center is a non-profit organization formed in 1996 with the mission of rehabilitating raptors. It consists of 29 acres of Valley Sanitary District land south of the treatment plant.

Valley Sanitary District dedicated the land to the Wild Bird Center and constructed a wetlands area that is integrated into its existing pond system. The wetlands "polish" wastewater by a natural biological process. The technique allows the District to achieve regulatory standards at a reduced cost and provides new wildlife habitat for the education and enjoyment of the public.

Future plans call for the Wild Bird Center to build an interpretive facility to introduce the public to the water reclamation and bird rehabilitation processes. Two local Indian tribes have expressed interest in the expansion plans, as their tribal lands are adjacent to the site. Tribal involvement would allow for additional open space for hiking, nature walks, and interpretive areas for native cultures.

The Great Outdoors

The City of Indio owns and operates a variety of leisure facilities. After 41 years of service, one of the best deals in town, day or night, is the Indio Municipal Golf Course. At 3,004 yards, it is the longest par 3 course in the country with an average hole length of 167 yards. And, as the only night-lighted course in the Valley, golfers can leisurely slip in 18 holes for only $15 even after a full day's work. Plans have been drawn to renovate and double in size the clubhouse and amenities. Extra yardage and water features are being designed on some holes.

Indio Community Center and Gymnasium.

The City of Indio owns 49 acres that has been set aside for use as parkland. Divided into eight locations, each park offers different amenities.

North Jackson Park: Night-lighted tennis courts, softball and baseball fields.

Terrace Park: 4.5 acres of open space. Plans are to add playground equipment.

Yucca Park: Basketball courts, new playground equipment is to arrive in 2005.

Dominguez Park on Monroe and Crown Way: Plans are under consideration for adding amenities to the open space.

Miles Avenue Park: Nearly 10 acres of the downtown revitalization project. Soccer and other fields, shade structures, restrooms and play equipment are being considered.

Dr. Carreon Park: The City hopes to receive grant funds from the State to renovate and convert the park for additional soccer fields.

South Jackson Park: New play equipment and shade structures are in place.

South Jackson Soccer Park: The 10-acre site is set to include four night-lighted soccer fields, playground equipment, shade structures, a concession stand and restrooms.

Desert Regional Park: 280 acres planned to be the home of the Coachella Valley Mounted Ranger Posse.

Coachella Valley Recreation and Park District programs attract more than half a million participants each year to take advantage of offerings like licensed after-school programs, sports tournaments and leagues, holiday celebrations, classes and special events. The District operates and maintains the 39,000-square-foot Indio Community Center & Gymnasium. Indio residents may use the facility that includes a fitness center and indoor running track for just $10 per year. The District also oversees Pawley Pool Swim and Fitness Center, which won the 2002 "Best Renovated Facility" award from the California Association of Recreation & Park Districts.

The Golden Age

The Indio Senior Center is a vibrant part of the downtown Civic Center where 150 seniors come for a variety of services and activities each weekday. The Center provides members with education enrichment, creative arts classes, and recreational opportunities. It is also their contact for advocacy, employment assistance, health and nutrition services, and a wide range of social services.

INDIO SENIOR CENTER

The Center's Meals on Wheels Program delivers an average of 40 specialized menu meals per day. A hot, catered lunch is served at the Center each Wednesday for $3.

Members can take in activities such as movies, day trips to popular attractions, bingo, bridge, quilting, ceramics, watercolors, stained glass, and crafts.

They can also take their AARP Mature Drivers Course or stay fit with exercise classes like TOPS (Taking Off Pounds Sensibly).

In 1976, the Riverside County Board of Supervisors in cooperation with the City of Indio took steps to fund and develop a senior citizen center. In 1978, seniors gained exclusive use of the former library building, and on May 12, 1980, dedication ceremonies were held for the new Indio Senior Center on Towne Street at the Civic Center mall.

Cornelia Jennings (97 years old) and MOW coordinator Alma Villalobos.

Bus trip to Lawrence Welk Village.

The need for a Senior Center was first realized in 1967. A couple of dozen members of AARP (American Association of Retired Persons) decided that the social interaction was so valuable that they should have a place where they and other seniors could meet five days a week.

By 1973, the federally funded Retired Senior Volunteer Program (RSVP) expanded across the valley and set up offices in Indio. One of RSVP's goals was to utilize older or retired adults to provide volunteer services at schools, libraries and nonprofit groups. According to a *Desert View* story dated May 20, 1976, senior volunteers contributed 25,687 hours of important effort in 1975 to 38 institutions in the Coachella Valley, meeting many of the social welfare needs of the region. "RSVP offers an opportunity to retire TO something rather than FROM something" quoted Helen Gillett, RSVP assistant director in 1978. During that time Indio had 124 volunteers performing functions in government and public offices and health programs.

In 1975, RSVP got involved with the Meals on Wheels project, providing food to Indio shut-ins. Initially, the food was prepared by Valley Memorial Hospital's kitchen. RSVP coordinated and provided volunteer drivers and the Indio Junior Women's Club screened intakes and provided bookkeeping duties.

The following year, RSVP added the "Daily Call" program to check up on people isolated due to illness, age, handicap or that are not in regular contact with friends or family. The "Indio Senior Information and Referral Service" directed seniors to available services for legal aid, housing, law enforcement, financial problems and health; and assistance completing tax forms.

Living History

They say that those who ignore history are doomed to repeat it. Textbooks can give you the facts, but eyewitnesses can give you the flavor. With this thought in mind, in 2004 Indio Senior Center Executive Director Dick Schroeder instituted a living history project called History Hunters.

Everyone is welcome to sit in while longtime residents (average tenure in the community is 60 years) discuss a topic relating to Indio's history. The group meets monthly to share memories about events, people and places from the past. Says Schroeder, "The beauty of the dynamic is that the seniors get to exercise their memory muscles while the observers get to re-live an experience they could never have gotten out of a book."

The popular group is chronicling Indio's image-rich past with their own colorful storytelling and personal photos. The Indio Senior Center staff is scanning old photos to catalog and preserve them in this on-going project.

THE 9/11 QUILT

Along with The Riverside County Fair & National Date Festival and Indio Sunrise Rotary Club, The Friends of the Indio Senior Center sponsored the three-day 9/11 Memorial Quilt Display, which was on a two-year tour across the country. The quilt, measuring five football fields long, memorializes each victim of the attacks on the World Trade Twin Towers, the Pentagon, and the passengers and crew of the American and United Airlines flights.

History Hunters meet once a month at the Indio Senior Center. Front row, left to right: June Hall, Lana Hall, Gloria Mendoza, Howard Mendoza, Evelyn Thompson and Lucille Cavanaugh. Second row: Bob Taylor, Marianne White, Beula Nyback, Virgina Paul, Lillan Williams, Ray House and Elmer Suski. Thrid Row: Walt /White, Earlene Oliver, Connie Cowan, Hazel Berghoeffer, Bob Williams, Bob Proco and Doug Cowan.

Passing The Torch

While Indio is mature in number of years incorporated, it has always been a youthful city in terms of the age of its residents. Youth are a big part of the community and one that the City of Indio recognizes as future consumers, businesspeople and civic leaders.

To address the exploding youth population in Indio in the late 1990s, the Indio Youth Task Force (IYTF) was formed. Its mission is to foster

City of Indio
Youth Advisory Council

networking between county agencies, youth organizations and social service providers as a means of juvenile intervention and education. The Task Force is funded by Community Development Block Grant monies and a $1 per ticket surcharge paid by Coachella Music

and Arts Festival patrons. The Task Force now represents over 70 organizations and hosts regular events for young people in the community.

In 1997, Mayor Mike Wilson implemented a youth advisory group to get the city's future residents involved in municipal government by offering their voice on important youth planning issues. Structured after the IYTF, the Indio Youth Advisory Council (IYAC) elects a Mayor who leads 11 other high school students who serve as Mayor Pro Tem, Secretary/Treasurer and council members. Members meet twice a month, attend and participate in city council meetings, and take part in the Indio Chamber of Commerce Mayor's Breakfasts and national youth planning conferences.

"Indio is far ahead of most cities just by having a Youth Planning Committee," reports 17-year-old Mayor Erika Green. "Indio is the only city in the Coachella Valley with an active youth council."

IYAC members serve the community by volunteering at events like the Tamale and Salsa Festivals, Fourth of July Fireworks and the American Cancer Society's Relay for Life charity walk. In 2003, IYAC started a paid internship program at the City and Indio Police Department.

The tangible work product that comes from the Indio Youth Advisory Committee is a Youth Master Plan. "In the works since 2002, the master plan is an ever-evolving framework of goals and objectives for serving Indio

youth and families," notes Indio Youth Coordinator and longtime valley resident Dave Ison. The youth counterparts to the sitting Indio City Council presents the blueprint to their elected officials for official endorsement. Both parties say they hope the plan will build a roadmap that will help young people grow up healthy, caring and responsible.

Left to right, Sherry Johnson, Pamper Rodriguez, Interim City Manager Ken Weller, Victoria Bailey, Mayor Melanie Fesmire and City Councilmember Ben Godfrey attending tree lighting ceremony.

YOUTH ADVISORY COUNCIL

As part of its youth advocacy outreach, the group successfully lobbied the Indio City Council to add a Youth Coordinator position to the City staff. Left to right, Lesley Rivas, Nicole Purdy, Anabel Castro, Roxanne Cota, Viviana Villarreal, Alan Huang, and Ingrid Rivas. Photo courtesy of Kiki Haynes.

TREE LIGHTING CEREMONY

Dick Schroeder and Linda Beal from the Indio Senior Center get in the spirit at the Indio tree lighting ceremony at City Hall.

A Place Of Their Own

Until 1990, the national organization to which the Indio Boy's Club was chartered did not include the word "girls." Since the time girls were added to the club's mix, the ratio of boys to girls participating in Indio Boys and Girls Club activities has been about 50-50. Within the past few years, the club was renamed again, this time to commemorate the fundraising drive of John Carroll and Jim O'Brien, who led the charge

to get the club up and running in the 1960s.

The John Carroll and Jim O'Brien Boys and Girls Club has provided career development opportunities for East Coachella Valley youth for more than 36 years with no plans to stop. With current membership nearing 750 children and teens, attendance climbs annually as innovative programs are added. As part of the 11-year, club-affiliated Building Horizons program, 25 students from both Desert Sands Unified and Coachella Valley Unified School Districts built a 4,500-square-foot Boxing Club addition. Since the ring opened in July 2004, 80 to 100 boys and girls train daily under role model and former world champion boxer, Antonio Diaz, who hails from neighboring Coachella.

Prominent Indio historical figure, Jackie Cochran, would be most proud of the club's innovative six-week program called "Reach for the Stars," which graduated its first three aviators in 2004. Members ages 15 to 18 learn about aviation and receive hands-on flying instruction that takes them to the point where they are ready for solo flights. The first participant in the program, 17-year-old Daniel Urrutia, is interested in joining the Air Force after becoming licensed by the FAA.

An additional 8,000-square-foot multipurpose Teen Center for ages 13 to 18 should be finished in 2006. The center will incorporate a music room where students may learn to play various instruments, a library of current reading material, a meeting room for guest lectures, a game room, and a cyber café. In tandem with Indio's Youth Master Plan, the center will also feature a full-service pizza restaurant. Youth members will prepare and serve food, perform bookkeeping, clean-up and maintenance functions to gain valuable employment training experience.

Shown here is volunteer Gladys Jaegers and some of the children at the John Carroll and Jim O'Brien Boys and Girls Club.

At top, Indio Boys & Girls Club Boxing and Athletic Center.

Reflections and Visions

Reflections are the product of careful consideration of an image. Vision helps us turn our reflections into dreams for the future. The collection of people, places and events documented in this book represents a mere snapshot of the many facets of Indio. Countless unsung heroes and everyday people continue to give Indio its depth of character and pursuit of excellence.

The vision for the future of Indio is one of boundless opportunities. This is a community of high energy and higher expectations for a rich and rewarding quality of life for its residents. The Indio of yesteryear laid a solid foundation for generations to come. Tomorrow's Indio promises to be a tapestry of many colors and textures that celebrates a hearty past and aspires to an even more remarkable future.

– Gayl Biondi, Editorial Director

Ode to Coachella Valley

By Edith Mann Ross

'Tis there the birds sing sweetest,
'Tis there the sun shines best,
Sweet verbenas bloom in profusion
In Coachella Valley, the land I love best.

Edith Mann Ross lived in a palm frond house on Fargo Avenue in Indio in 1896. Her poem attests to her love of this place and her own acceptance and appreciation of life.

EARLY 1900s

COACHELLA VALLE
ICE & COLD-S

Profiles
of Excellence

*Historic Mural: History of the Electricity,
corner of Civic Center Drive and
Fargo Street, artist Jim Fanestock,
completed in 2000.*

ABC Recovery Center

*A*BC Recovery Center has been part of the Indio landscape for more than 40 years. The peer-oriented, social model recovery home and detoxification facility gets results through proven 12-step programs, professional counseling and positive peer pressure. Treatments begin with a 90-day minimum stay in the Primary Care Facility followed by transition to the Sober Living Facilities where residents gain skills that will enable them to reenter the community as healthy and responsible adults.

The center had its beginnings in an adobe house on Miles Avenue. The cost was $7 a week for a place to sleep and $13 a week included two meals a day. There was room for eight people.

John Peters, a prominent Indio citizen, later donated a two-story house which was moved to Biskra Street. This became the ABC Club which was incorporated in 1963.

Danny Leahy was named manager in 1970. Shortly thereafter he and his bride, Helen, started co-managing the club. They have been there ever since and today oversee a staff of 25 on an 11-acre campus. Today they provide a caring environment for substance abuse recovery for as many as 150 adults and children at any given time.

"Everybody gets an opportunity to recover," says Helen. If one can't afford to pay, there are county beds and an adopt-a-bed program funded from

> **"Residents gain skills that will enable them to reenter the community as healthy and responsible adults."**

Recovery Center

ABC's furniture store Leather Plus, a 20,000-square-foot store in Old Town Indio. A generous benefactor on a regular basis donates new, top quality leather furniture and this is supplemented by donated furnishings from residents in the community. In addition to funds from state and federal grants, the non-profit organization presents its Ambassador Leonard K. Firestone Award of Merit at its annual fundraiser.

Monies go toward a number of programs including: After Care - provides continuing care to those with 90 days of residential treatment and others in recovery. Family - supports families to identify and express feelings. Perinatal - expectant and postpartum mothers receive parenting training and newborns are allowed to stay in residence with their mothers. Educational Support - allows residents to prepare for further schooling through peer tutoring. Youth Outreach - residents, staff and alumni speak to young people about addiction.

Support comes through gifts of cash as well as non-cash gifts which include stocks, bonds, securities and real estate. Donors are urged to contact their legal, tax or other professional advisors on all matters of charitable giving.

For more information: 760-342-6616 or www.abcrecovery.com

The Ames Group

Paul Ames believes in cycles. Whether it's the seasons or the tides, this Indio agriculture and real estate pioneer understands the patterns of life's ups and downs. Quips Ames, "We should all expect to have at least three really great moments and the same number of really bad moments in our lives, and I've known them all. The best hope is to wind up on a good one."

One of the Ames Family's truly defining moments came before Paul's birth, when, in 1914, his grandfather picked up a real estate brochure promoting the dream of Mecca, a sort of agricultural suburb of Indio. It promised a year-round climate and fertile land on a railroad to deliver the produce to market. The elder Ames sold his grocery store to stake an 80-acre spread and dug an Artesian well. He set up a tent with no electricity and leveled the land with a team of horses.

In 1930, Paul's father, George, carried on with the business, perfecting the process of icing Sweet Corn. Paul was born and reared on the family farm but left to fly airplanes in World War II and go on to earn a college degree. His graduation coincided with the opening of the All-American Canal, which brought vital Colorado River water to the east end of the Coachella Valley. With this promise of new water and new land, Paul's pioneer genes kicked in.

Thus confirmed Paul Ames' love affair with what he calls "the green end of the Coachella Valley." Even though Paul was a creative farmer, he hedged his bets with entrepreneurial ventures including Palco Linings, his own invention of durable plastic liners for manmade lakes and reservoirs. He also launched a real estate sales and development business. "Farming and real estate have a lot in common; they both involve dirt," Paul observes.

Paul Ames has watched Indio move through its own cycles over the past 75 years. He recalls the 1980s when agriculture was in a slump, the railroad had moved its operations to Colton, and Interstate 10 bypassed the business district. Looking at the city today, he is pleased to see the way Indio is upgrading its housing and retail offerings. His company, The Ames Group, is actively expanding its brokerage and land development activities. He and Indio are enjoying this cycle of life. Says Paul with a smile, "2005 is truly an Up Cycle for Indio and for me."

For more information: 760-345-2555

> "Looking at the city today, he is pleased to see the way Indio is upgrading its housing and retail offerings."

Best Western Date Tree Hotel

It is one of the oldest hotels in Indio, having its origins in the late 1950s. Back then the property was known as The Hacienda. In 1972, it became the Best Western Date Tree Hotel, and in 2002 the franchise was purchased by Alice and Jason Shaw.

The Shaws, who reside in Los Angeles, fell in love with Indio during one of their many visits to the Coachella Valley. "The couple has a very definite idea of how to treat people," says Aaron Segal, general manager of the Best Western Date Tree Hotel. Their philosophy and Segal's is to focus on the employee first.

"It's really quite simple," says Segal, whose company, AltaMont Hotels, Inc., manages the hotel. "If you don't provide an enriching environment for your associates, you can't expect them to take care of guests properly."

Associates are rewarded for their loyalty with competitive wages and a health care package that is remarkable for small hotels. Indeed, after five years of employment, there is no out-of-pocket cost to the employee for heath insurance.

It is in this stimulating atmosphere of teamwork that the property continues to flourish. After more than 15 years in the hospitality industry, Segal, who joined the hotel and AltaMont in 2002, is well aware of the unique amenities offered guests.

Located on 5 1/2 acres dotted with citrus

> "It is in this stimulating atmosphere of teamwork that the property continues to flourish."

trees, the hotel has an Olympic-sized swimming pool with a whirlpool spa. Guest rooms are extraordinarily spacious. In fact, five of the eight suites boast a full kitchen complete with stove, microwave and refrigerator. And, each suite has a whirlpool tub in the master bedroom.

In keeping with the hotel's name, arriving guests are greeted with complimentary dates and freshly baked cookies. Breakfast is also complimentary and includes fruit, juices and pastries available in a sunny space just off the lobby. There is even a DVD library of more than 300 movies that guests can choose from and watch at no charge in the comfort of their rooms.

Segal is excited about Indio's growth and the beautiful renovation of Indio Boulevard. He attributes the success of the community to the hard work of visionary people who have a passion for a promising future. An active member of the Indio Chamber of Commerce, Segal has been on the board of directors and served as chairman of the Tourism Committee.

"Every day there is something new to look forward to."

For more information: 760-347-3421 or www.datetree.com

J he Boys Club of Coachella Valley opened its Indio facility in December 1966. A group of visionary people had a novel approach to fundraising. Contributions to the building fund could be no less than $500, which could be paid over a five-year period if necessary. Membership to the club would be $1 a year, but if that was too steep for some it could be paid by helping with the construction.

"It got started the right way," says Jim Ducatte, chief professional officer, who has been with the organization since 1982. "Our founders were extremely dedicated and we've been able to maintain that enthusiasm and keep people involved over the years."

In 1990 the organization changed its name to the Boys & Girls Club of Coachella Valley, welcoming girls to participate. Today, in addition to the Jim O'Brien and John Carroll Boys and Girls Club of Indio facility, there are clubhouses in La Quinta and Coachella, which serve a total of more than 4,000 members between the ages of 7 and 18.

The Boys & Girls Club of Coachella Valley's unique programs include: Building Horizons - a collaborative program with local school districts and the building industry that trains high school juniors and seniors in construction skills. To date, more than 400 students have completed 25 low- and moderate-income homes, as well as a 4,400 square foot Boxing

> "Our founders were extremely dedicated and we've been able to maintain enthusiasm and keep people involved."

BOYS & GIRLS CLUB
OF COACHELLA VALLEY

and Athletic Center addition at the Indio clubhouse.

"Reach for the Stars" Aviation Program - the only Boys & Girls Club program in the country where select teens ages 15-18 learn about aviation and receive hands-on flying instruction. Based out of the Bermuda Dunes Airport, the six-week program is conducted in cooperation with Twin Palms Aviation.

The Valley's Promise - partnering with Leadership Coachella Valley and 14 Coachella Valley high schools, this teen program creates tomorrow's leaders. LINKS - a collaborative program that focuses on youth who are experiencing difficulties with academics, family and/or peer relationships. All-American Youth Golf teaches the basics of golf through individual and team play. Boxing Club, at the new state-of-the-art Boxing and Athletic Center in Indio, instructors focus on physical conditioning and competitive boxing, as well as classes in karate and dance.

The organization's fresh approach continues with plans for a 7,000 square foot Teen Center, scheduled for completion in 2006, adjacent to their Indio facility. The center will focus on educational and career development programs specifically for teens.

For more information: 760-836-1160 of www.bgcofcv.org.

Boys & Girls Club of Coachella Valley

City of Indio

In the past few years, many words have been attributed to the City of Indio: booming, phenomenal and unprecedented are just a few. Indio is the oldest and largest city in the Coachella Valley and its resurgence as a major force among desert communities has now become part of its rich history.

Native Americans first settled along the San Andreas Fault in the Indio Hills and along the Whitewater River. The Cahuilla society had an estimated population of between 6,000 and 10,000. In the late 1700s, Spanish and Mexican exploratory and military expeditions, miners and settlers traveled through the area using the San Gorgonio pass on route to their destinations.

Surveyors from the Southern Pacific Railroad chose the Indio area as a suitable location for a railroad depot noting it was a halfway point between Yuma and Los Angeles and that there was sufficient construction labor available from the Indian reservations. Trains began running from Los Angeles to Indio in 1876 and a year later the route to Yuma was completed.

When Indio incorporated as a city in 1930 it had a population of 1,875. With the construction of the All American Canal, the agricultural industry began to mushroom with subsequent growth in retail, tourism and, of course, population.

"The city has developed at different speeds

> "Today the City of Indio is proudly celebrating its 75th Anniversary. The city's current population of 59,100 is expected to double by 2010."

over time but the present time is the most dramatic," says Mayor Melanie Fesmire. Today the City of Indio is proudly celebrating its 75th Anniversary. The city's current population of 59,100 is expected to double by 2010. "The city is now embarking on a new phase and it is moving forward in a positive manner to once again take its leadership role in the Coachella Valley," says Ken Weller, interim city manager.

Currently there are approximately 25,000 entitled homes that have received city council approval and are expected to be built in the next few years. To put a perspective on the amazing growth, between 2002 and 2004 the total valuation of new buildings constructed more than doubled to $487,835,878 in 2004.

Indeed the housing market has been so hot in

Indio that it was not unusual to hear of phases being sold out before model homes were started and waiting lists for homes in the hundreds.

According to Weller, the attraction for developers has been the availability of large parcels of land, affordability and what the community has to offer in terms of lifestyle.

"We have raised the bar on quality housing and can compete with any Valley city," says Ben Godfrey, city council member. Prospective homeowners can look forward to bigger homes and bigger lots - a marked difference from the gated-community condominiums that flourished in the early 1980s. Buyers looking to upgrade or to invest in a primary home in a family-oriented city have found Indio to be the happy solution.

"Indio has an environment that offers an opportunity to work, play and live. From recreation, entertainment (via festivals), variety in restaurants and peaceful serenity, Indio has it all," says Lupe Ramos Watson, city council member.

Indio is called the "City of Festivals" and in conjunction with the Indio Chamber of Commerce is renowned for multi-cultural festivals which include the Riverside County Fair & National Date Festival, the International Salsa Festival, the Southwest Arts Festival, the International Tamale Festival, Coachella Music and Arts Festival, Indio Desert Circuit Horse Show and the Native American Powwows.

Another signature of the community is its beautiful murals which grace many of the buildings around Old Town and on Indio Boulevard. These historic murals give a glimpse of the Golden State's past not only by their renderings but location as well. Indio Boulevard was part of US 99 which was commissioned in 1926 and ran from the Canadian border south to the Mexican border. Indio is often touted as a city with a rich past and a dynamic future.

"The future for the City of Indio is nothing short of bright and extremely successful," says Michael Wilson, city council member. The key will be the continuity of the policy makers and staff working diligently together. With the priorities of keeping our community safe through a high standard for public safety and meeting quality of life issues of our residents with open space, parks and recreational opportunities for our youth population, the city is poised to become the premier city in the Valley." The City Council had an eye on the future when it re-established the Redevelopment Agency three years ago. They wanted to have a strategy in place when development began moving eastward.

CITY OF INDIO

"Any development proposal has an effect on the environment in a community. The best projects are those that are sensitive to everything around them. They are such that they take into consideration the entire fabric of the community," explains Rudy Acosta, director of redevelopment/economic development.

"It's all about smart development."

For more information: 760-342-6500 or www.indio.org

Photo by Ruben Diaz

Clark's Travel Center

Bruce Clark has not only created a convenient one-stop-shopping complex, but an experience. For more than three decades, he and his wife, Dolores, have been providing superb customer service and a touch of Indio history to residents and travelers who stop by Clark's Travel Center.

Two stunning murals representing Indio's transportation in the 1920s and 1930s are the first colorful surprises to catch motorists' attention. They are among seven displayed throughout the community in a privately funded chamber project initiated by Clark.

The history of transportation is also part of Clark's Travel Center's history for it is the oldest operating truckstop on Historic Route 99. Although it is called Indio Boulevard today, in 1926 it was commissioned as US 99 and linked Mexicali, Mexico, through the states of California, Oregon and Washington, to Vancouver, Canada. Towns and businesses flourished along these corridors; however, with the advent of the Interstate system, traffic bypassed these areas in favor of faster transportation.

Literally, the signs of these times can be seen today at Clark's Travel Center's museum. Clark has been collecting primarily porcelain

> "Literally, the signs of these times can be seen today at Clark's Travel Center's museum."

CLARK'S TRAVEL CENTER

signs for more than 30 years. His collection dates back to the early 1900s and reveals his passion for Union Oil signage. When it comes to license plates, he has porcelain plates made prior to 1919 from every state. Highway 99 memorabilia also has a special place in the museum with signs, pictures and maps promoting the historic route.

Clark's Travel Center is open 24/7 with reasonably priced gas, diesel and racing fuel. There is a convenience store, self-serve and drive-thru car wash that can accommodate RVs and trucks, a Mexican restaurant open 24 hours a day, and a card-op laundry. "With major truckstops built on the freeway we had to change," explains Clark.

"At one time we were the largest tire dealer in the Coachella Valley. We had road service trucks and mechanics on duty 24 hours a day. In fact, in 1980 we were listed among the top 10 truckstops in the country in a customer survey conducted by Union Oil."

Today the tire and mechanical side of the business has closed, replaced by Clark's convenience store. And the good news is that with the boom in new home construction, Indio Boulevard is as busy as ever.

"My dad always told me that history repeats itself," says Clark.

For more information: 760-342-4776 or www.clarkstravelcenter.com.

Coachella Valley Printing Group

COACHELLA VALLEY PRINTING GROUP INC.

John Edwards, owner of the Coachella Valley Printing Group, is delighted with his company's Indio location.

In 1990 he purchased Arrow Printing which had been doing business in Indio since 1969. Ever the entrepreneur, Edwards expanded his operation by acquiring a number of small, local printing companies. Today Coachella Valley Printing Group, which occupies the former Daily News building on Towne Street, is the largest printing facility in the Coachella Valley with more than two dozen employees.

Edwards' personal story is equally as fascinating. A native of England, he came to the United States in 1989. Prior to coming to this country, he spent 15 years in the Middle East and Africa. During this time he was an air traffic controller and a director of the international airport at Salalah, Oman. When he returned to England, he got his first exposure to the world of printing through an advertising franchise he purchased.

Three years later and with a fondness for warm weather, he found himself in the printing business in the Coachella Valley. Edwards not only immersed himself in his growing business but in the community as well. Today he is actively involved in local charities often sponsoring such cultural events as the La Quinta Arts Foundation's annual Desert Plein Air Invitational. In addition, Coachella Valley

> **"The largest printing facility in the Coachella Valley with more than two dozen employees."**

Printing Group often discounts its services to nonprofit organizations that reap the dual benefits of quality and value. In fact, a recent La Quinta Arts Foundation's festival poster printed by Edwards' company was the recipient of a *Sunrise Magazine* award of excellence.

Edwards believes that his company's success is based on having good people on his team, employing efficiencies and keeping abreast of the latest technology. And of course, one-on-one client communication and incomparable customer service is a given.

His company produces everything from business cards to elaborate four-color catalogues. Coachella Valley Printing Group boasts the largest sheet-fed press in the desert. They also have a thermographer which enables them to produce "embossed-like" invitations, announcements and stationery at a fraction of the cost. Clients include the City of Palm Desert, Bighorn Country Club and El Dorado Polo. Local casinos have increasingly looked to the Coachella Valley Printing Group to provide a myriad of collateral for their operations.

"Indio - we're in a great place at a great time," says Edwards.

For more Information: 760-347-7316.

Design Collections and Upholstery Outlet

*L*ook out Old Town. Carolyn French and Bill Tanghe, husband and wife proprietors of Design Collections & Upholstery Outlet, have exciting plans for their Indio business.

After almost 20 years at various locations in the Coachella Valley, the enterprising couple has found the perfect spot. In 1986, with $600 in the bank, they opened The Upholstery Outlet, a 600-square-foot store in Palm Springs. Five expansions and seven years later they moved to a 6,500-square-foot store in Cathedral City where they added The Design Collections and prospered for the next 10 years. In 2002, they bought a 7,500-square-foot building on Miles Avenue in Old Town, refurbishing it completely and adding an attractive Spanish Colonial façade. They recently purchased an adjacent building with plans for further expansion.

"Our goal is to be the kingpin in restoring Old Town to a destination shopping and cultural center," says Tanghe.

Design Collections & Upholstery Outlet is famous for it tremendous selection of fabrics. It has more than 70,000 hanging sample fabrics, a library of sample books and some 500 roles of fabric. The store is also known for its unique collection of one-of-a-kind pieces of Colonial, Old World and Mexican furniture and accessories.

> **"Design Collections and Upholstery Outlet, have exciting plans for their Indio business."**

"We try to find things that are unusual. Many of our pieces come from the interior of Mexico. For instance, we have a 16-foot cabinet from a grocery store and another owned by Pancho Villa's daughter," says Tanghe.

But that's not all. After 20 years of collecting they have accumulated many treasures that aren't for sale, but are on display high on the store's walls. "We tell people to plan on staying an hour or two. And when they come back they always see something they hadn't noticed before," says Tanghe. Tanghe likes to quote the saying: Happiness is doing what you like and liking what you do.

French's family was in interior design and she attended the Art Institute in Chicago, while Tanghe has a background in home improvement. Little wonder that their enthusiasm which began with the design of little foot stools has mushroomed into the beautiful store they have today.

The community agrees. They are two-time recipients of the City of Indio/Indio Chamber of Commerce Image Award. In addition, Tanghe has been invited to serve on the Chamber's Board of Directors.

Look out Old Town. Design Collections & Upholstery Outlet is on the grow.

For more information: 760-342-7887

Eaton & Kirk Advertising

When Eaton & Kirk Advertising opened its doors 15 years ago, the husband and wife team of Emmie Lou Eaton and John Kirkpatrick had good reasons for choosing Indio.

"We recognized the tremendous potential of this community and that it wouldn't be long before growth moved eastward," said Kirkpatrick.

While the firm has prospered over the years and now has a staff of six, its core philosophy of providing personalized service remains its hallmark. While Eaton focuses on the administrative side of the operation, Kirkpatrick works one-on-one with clients providing a full-service range of advertising, design, marketing and internet development services.

Kirkpatrick is skilled in design, illustration, photography and copy enabling him to give clients simultaneous attention to all details of advertising and marketing. As for his education, Kirkpatrick says, "I took the Renaissance guy approach." With a scholarship in engineering, Kirkpatrick attended Carnegie Mellon in Pittsburgh where he triple-majored in engineering, architecture and art. With a propensity toward the fine arts, he soon found himself at the California Institute of the Arts in Valencia where he concentrated on art and design. This led to a five-year stint at Otis College of Art & Design in Los Angeles where he taught design, production and typography.

> "We recognized the tremendous potential of this community and that it wouldn't be long before growth moved eastward."

EATON & KIRK
ADVERTISING • MARKETING
WEB SITE DEVELOPMENT

Kirkpatrick's extensive background was instrumental in guiding his firm into the forefront of cutting edge technology. Eaton & Kirk Advertising has its own dedicated server for website hosting with support supplied by one of the industry's leading internet firms. Eaton & Kirk is renowned for its emphasis on the interactivity of the websites it designs and is considered a leader in e-marketing services and custom programming.

Among its client base are regional and local developers, realtors, hotels, restaurants, utilities and civic organizations. Clients include Landmark Golf Club, The Living Desert Zoo & Gardens and the Coachella Valley Enterprise Zone. In addition, the firm has worked with the cities of Indio and Coachella as well as chambers of commerce in Indio, La Quinta and Borrego Springs. In fact, the visual concepts and graphic design for *Indio Reflections and Visions* were created by Eaton & Kirk.

Most of its clients are long-term such as the legendary Melvyn's Restaurant and the Ingleside Inn which have been with Eaton & Kirk for over a dozen years. "For us it's about investing in the client and delivering extraordinary creative results on time and within budget," says Kirkpatrick.

For more information: 760-775-3626 or www.eatonkirk.com

Events by Joe Scarna, Inc.

Joe Scarna knows how to throw a party. With a background in business banking and a love of the theater, Scarna has managed to meld the two into a successful operation that has achieved national acclaim.

Events by Joe Scarna was created in 1999. Active in the Palm Springs Community Theater as both an actor and set designer, Scarna was asked to apply his talents to a corporate event being planned by his wife, Allyson's employer, Brier & Dunn California, a destination management company located in Palm Desert. After six months of designing and building, Scarna built a Titanic set that is still talked about today.

The event, which was held at the Empire Polo Club, had guests dining in the Titanic's exquisite ballroom when they were forced to evacuate into small lifeboats while the ship, with the sounds of a symphony in the background, sunk.

"Our character and ethical beliefs are a major part of our creative force in every event we produce," says Scarna. "By giving our clients the best of service and living up to our designs beyond their expectations, we have the edge we need to stay ahead of the curve. Keeping everything we do fresh and exciting is no easy task, but we have been able to accomplish our creative goals through education and the sharing of ideas within our company and among our peers. Strict standards and never compromising is a way of life here at Events by Joe Scarna."

> "Our character and ethical beliefs are a major part of our creative force in every event we produce."

Located at the old Yellow Mart site on Towne and Miles in Indio, Scarna's company brings experience, innovation and a well-stocked toolbox full of event design and production services to any event. This includes lighting equipment from fiber optic curtains and moving lights to theater lighting. There are audiovisual services that can complete a stage set for any band. Events by Joe Scarna's floral department creates up to 300 centerpieces a week and the company is renowned for its custom designed table linens of unique textiles.

In fact, Toll Brothers commissioned Scarna to create "The Perfect Setting," Thanksgiving tablescape designs that were on display in eight model homes.

Themes included "Like a Fine Wine," "Sante Fe Style" and "Pilgrimage."

"The way a table is set creates the tone and ambiance for a meal, especially when it's a holiday with special family and friends included," says Scarna.

Scarna's company also participates in local parades. It has won a Theme Trophy in the Palm Desert Golf Cart Parade and was commissioned by the Palm Springs Aerial Tramway to build a float for the City's 12th Annual Festival of Lights Parade. This float depicted a rotating tramcar overlooking the San Jacinto Mountains and Chino Canyon. It bested more than 100 entrants winning the 1st Place Sweepstakes Trophy.

After September 11, 2001, Events by Joe Scarna found it necessary to branch out, and float design and building was one of the directions it took. Today, the company receives requests from throughout Southern California to create floats. It has also added a wedding division and is proud to be a part of this growing industry.

Requests for Scarna's expertise have gone way beyond the local and regional scope. He is asked to lecture on design at Special Events Conferences often attended by more than 350 industry professionals. Not long ago he was asked to make a presentation to designers attending a National Association of Catering Executives Conference in San Antonio. Events by Joe Scarna is also a member of Team Net, an organization that refers it to clients throughout the world that might have need of its services.

Scarna attributes much of his company's success to its technology and the software that Go forth Technology has designed for them.

> "Requests for Scarna's expertise have gone way beyond the local and regional scope."

"With two and three shows a day, the details are enormous," says Scarna. "This software allows us to make changes in real time. Each employee's phone is automatically dialed when a change is made and the change can be viewed on a text message as well as on the Web site. It has kept our company on the cutting edge allowing us to handle more events and even more complicated programs without missing a boat. It allows us to be creative and not so overwhelmed by the

many details involved in our events, weddings and private parties."

With 40,000 square feet of production studio, warehouse and office space, Events by Joe Scarna is well equipped to handle some 300 events a year. An active member of the

Indio Chamber of Commerce, Scarna is delighted to be part of Indio's exciting future.

"We are very proud to be part of a City that is working as hard as we are to 'Catch the Vision, something every company and resident should be trying to accomplish."

For more information: 760-347-8881 or www.eventsbyjoescarna.com

Fantasy Springs Resort Casino

Surveying the panoramic view of the Coachella Valley from the stunning 12th-floor Sunset View lounge brings the Fantasy Springs Resort vision into perfect focus. The magnificent new 250-room luxury hotel and 100,000-square-foot special events and entertainment center are the cornerstones of future growth and development for a resourceful people determined to maintain their sovereignty and self-determination.

The Cabazon Indians made history on October 2nd, 1980 with the opening of the first commercial card room on an Indian Reservation, and again in 1983 with the first high-stakes Indian Bingo operation in the state. In 2004, the tribe upped the ante by becoming the first in California and only the second in the U.S. to use a tax-exempt conduit bond issue to fund the expansion of a tribal business enterprise.

According to John A. James, Cabazon Tribal Chairman, "The hotel and Special Events Center represent a shift for the Cabazon Band of Mission Indians in the way we've been building an organization that benefits the long-standing outlook for the tribe. We have poured an enormous amount of capital into creating something that benefits the community as well, in terms of job creation, economic expansion

FANTASY SPRINGS
RESORT CASINO
CASINO · SPECIAL EVENTS CENTER · HOTEL

and growth for the cities of Indio and Coachella. This has always been the tribe's home, and we're happy to see that we can help create a thriving community for others as well."

The Fantasy Springs Resort hotel is the tallest structure in the Coachella Valley and the first in the valley connected to a casino. Full-service amenities include high-speed Internet access in every room, flat-screen TVs with in-room movies on demand, 24-hour room service, swimming and soaking pools, a retail shopping concourse, and a wide array of dining options.

Fantasy Springs Resort Casino offers up more than 100,000 square feet of upscale casino gaming and entertainment. Options include 2,000 of the newest slot machines available, a 750-seat Bingo Palace with smoking and non-smoking sections as well as a snack bar and off-track satellite wagering in the club-like Triple Crown Room. Table games run the gamut from Double-Deck Pitch Blackjack and Poker to mini-Baccarat, Spanish 21, Pai Gow, California craps and Video roulette.

Even food and beverage are taken to a higher level at Fantasy Springs Resort. The Springs Bar features 44 bar-top slots along with 12 plasma screen TVs. Players Steakhouse is

> "With the opening of the sparkling new resort hotel complex, the fantasy has only just begun."

completely remodeled with hardwood floors, flagstone walls, leather chairs and contemporary artwork to surround guests with elegance. A new 250-seat international buffet and poolside bistro-style eatery round out the dining options.

Not everyone who beats a path to Fantasy Springs is looking for a lucky hand. Some are looking for a lucky strike – as in bowling a perfect game. The 24-lane, state-of-the-art Fantasy Lanes Family Bowling Center is visited by 10,000 people each month. The center plays host to multiple daytime and nighttime leagues and a premier junior bowler program. A destination in its own right, the bowling center also sports a snack bar, video arcade, pro shop, cocktail lounge and party planner. Future plans call for an expansion to 60 lanes.

Constructed by the same company that built the Seattle Space Needle, the Fantasy Springs Resort special events center can accommodate up to 4,500 people for concerts, sporting events, banquets, trade shows, conventions and other group functions. The location is proving to be a draw for regional business meetings with its high-tech telecommunications capabilities and flexible, modular design. A 2,400-space parking structure will complement the center's myriad uses in 2005.

With the opening of the sparkling new resort hotel complex, the fantasy has only just begun. Future development phases are planned to bring additional recreation opportunities to the eastern Coachella Valley. The Cabazons have drafted an ambitious master plan that includes a second resort hotel with up to 400 rooms, a timeshare resort, an 18-hole golf course, a destination shopping center, an expansive day spa and a tribal administration and cultural center.

Says James H. McKennon, Fantasy Springs Resort Chief Executive Officer, "The Cabazons have a long history here in the valley of building from the ground up. The resort is a perfect example of the tribe's commitment to diversifying the area's revenue base while enhancing Indio's destination brand."

Club Fantasy, the desert's most popular player's club, counts an estimated 250,000 members who enjoy earning rewards and member-only events and incentives. Even casual players are calling Fantasy Springs "Party Central" thanks to festive holiday celebrations for St. Patrick's Day, Cinco de Mayo, Halloween and New Year's Eve.

The Cabazon Band of Mission Indians marks its heritage with a celebration of song, dance and culture at the Indio Powwow held Thanksgiving weekend and the on-site Cabazon Cultural Museum. From high atop the Sunset View lounge on the 12th floor to the drum cadence connecting tribal dancers to the earth during the Powwow, there is plenty to celebrate at Fantasy Springs Resort Casino.

For more information: 800-827-2946 or www.fantasyspringsresort.com

Granite Construction Company

Since 1922, Granite Construction Company has provided civil construction services and construction materials such as rock, sand and asphalt to the public sector as well as private companies and owners. Headquartered in Watsonsville, Calif., the firm is organized into two operating divisions.

The Heavy Construction Division focuses on major infrastructure projects throughout the United States while the Branch Division is made up of offices serving local markets. The company's Southern California Branch has been in the Coachella Valley since 1992, when it purchased the mining and construction operation from Tarmac. Headquartered in the Palm Springs Area Office in Indio, with additional offices in El Centro and yucca Valley, it is dedicated to building infrastructure projects - roads, bridges, sewer, water and drainage systems - in Southern California, and is the largest construction aggregate mining operation in the Coachella Valley.

GRANITE CONSTRUCTION COMPANY SINCE 1922

Part of the company's success can be attributed to its practice of allowing its branch managers to make sound business decisions on a local level. This is significant in the construction business where projects need to move forward without delay.

And with Indio's extraordinary increase in residential and commercial construction, it becomes even more significant. "The future is bright. As the

> "The largest construction aggregate mining operation in the Coachella Valley."

Coachella Valley has grown, our volume of business has grown right along with it," says Jay L. McQuillen, Jr., branch manager. "It is my belief that a rising tide floats all boats and that includes Granite. We are uniquely situated to take advantage of that growth."

Granite is at the cutting edge of technology with an in-house quality control lab, certified by Caltrans and national certifying agencies and under the direction of a registered engineering geologist. The company is the leader in rubber asphalt projects in the Coachella Valley, using recycled tires to build a smoother, quieter road system. And in Imperial County, Granite has been recognized for its innovative concrete ditch lining, a boon to farmers seeking to irrigate more efficiently.

Granite Construction Incorporated, the parent company of Granite Construction Company, is a member of the S&P 400 Index. Its accomplishments and way of doing business have not gone unnoticed. It has been the recipient of numerous awards including being named to FORTUNE magazine's list of the "100 Best Companies to Work For in America."

Employees are encouraged to participate in community and professional organizations. It is all part of the company's culture which celebrates pride, professionalism and responsibility as its trademarks.

For more information: 760-775-7500 or www.graniteconstruction.com

Guy Evans, Inc.

GUY EVANS, INC.
"Dedicated to the Finish"

Guy Evans has come home to Indio. In 1978 he and his wife, Malia, started their finish carpentry business out of their Indio home and began building doors, windows and relationships in the custom, commercial and tract construction industries.

Today, 26 years, 600 employees, and thousands of projects later, Guy Evans, Inc. (GEI) has relocated from Thousand Palms back to Indio, to a 28-acre parcel just off Interstate 10 and Jackson Avenue. Located in the campus-style industrial park called The Spectrum at Shadow Hills, the 100,000-square-foot, first-of-five buildings is home to GEI corporate headquarters and the company's Commercial, Production, Manufacturing, Custom, Design and Contractor Showroom divisions.

"Indio is a great city," says Evans. "The people are a pleasure to work with, they demonstrate their support through the city's incentives for locating in Enterprise and Empowerment Zones, which made it financially smart for our growing company to relocate."

Growth has been a constant for GEI from the beginning. The company has built an outstanding team and developed strong relationships with builders throughout Southern California and Nevada. Now, in addition to the Indio corporate headquarters, GEI has offices in Riverside, San Diego, Las Vegas and El Centro, providing doors, millwork, builder's hardware, windows and finish carpentry for a broad spectrum of homes. GEI's slogan is "Dedicated to the Finish" and all divisions work closely with clients to

> "Growth has been a constant for Guy Evans, Inc. from the beginning."

provide innovative solutions and to plan, budget, schedule and manage projects from start to finish.

The Production Division supports tract homebuilders by supplying and professionally installing doors, millwork, builder's hardware, trim, cabinetry and windows. The Custom Division works with architects, designers and builders to provide finishing touches such as specialty doors and lift and slides as well as hardware, cabinetry, millwork, trim and windows. The Commercial Division fabricate, provide and install hollow-metal and wood doors, frames, windows, architectural hardware and accessories for institutional, high-rise, specialty-use, governmental, military, office and industrial projects. In the Manufacturing Division, experienced craftsmen fabricate custom doors, architectural millwork, cabinetry and closets for builders and homeowners.

The new Design and Contractor Showroom provides a gallery-like setting for displays of doors, hardware, high-end plumbing fixtures, closet systems, architectural millwork, specialties and windows. It is open to individual homeowners, designers and local finish contractors. From a small carpentry business to one of the largest suppliers of custom, commercial and residential building products, Guy Evans, Inc. has come full circle. Its roots and its future are in Indio.

For more information: 760-343-1299 or www.guyevans.com

Horse Shows In The Sun

The Indio Desert Circuit is definitely a win-win-win for the city, participants and spectators. Since 1992, Horse Shows In The Sun, Inc. (HITS), the largest producer of show jumping competitions in the United States, has been dazzling the desert and equestrian communities with a six-week spectacular that attracts more than 10,500 horsemen and some 3,500 horses.

Although more than 25,000 fans watch the competition which is held at the 80-acre HITS Desert Horse Park, the benefits are even more far reaching in that Indio has become well-known to equestrians worldwide. And, it is estimated that the impact on the local economy exceeds $121 million.

"Of the five horse show circuits we produce around the country, Indio is our largest," says John Eickman, HITS National Marketing Director. "Our participants represent one of the richest demographics of any sports market and Indio is a popular venue. Actually, the weather makes it a near perfect location."

Some of the wealthiest people in the country descend upon Indio during the first quarter of each year for six consecutive weeks of the largest hunter/jumper competition west of the Mississippi. There are more than 300 different classes of competition for jumpers and hunters held in 10 competition rings. Horsemen vie for $1 million in prize money that comes from

Indio DESERT CIRCUIT

entries and stabling fees as well as sponsorships. The Ford Grand Prix of the Desert, which is held on the final show day, has $150,000 in prize money alone.

Local charities also benefit through ticket pre-sales and by volunteering as ticket-takers on weekends. Charity partners such as the Boys & Girls Club of the Coachella Valley, Boy Scouts of America, Indio Chamber of Commerce, Indio Senior Center, Coachella Rotary and the City of Indio Police Cadets combined reap 50% of the proceeds for their efforts.

HITS is the brainchild of Tom Struzzieri, who started out as a trainer teaching youngsters how to ride. Today he is president of this nationwide special events management company which produces hunter/jumper shows in California, Florida, Arizona, New York and Virginia. Headquartered in Saugerties, New York, the company is renowned for providing competitive opportunities for riders in a broad range of age and skill levels. With a focus on keeping the United States in the forefront of the industry, HITS offers more internationally sanctioned competitions than any other producer of horse shows.

For more information: 845-246-8833 or www.hitsshows.com

> "Of the five horse show circuits we produce around the country, Indio is our largest."

Imperial Sign Co.

Since 1961, Indio-based Imperial Sign has been serving the Coachella Valley and High Desert communities.

Call it a family affair. Ralph Engle opened his shop on Calhoun Street and a year later he was joined by his then 19-year-old son, Jim, who has been on the job since. Along the way Jim took time to marry Ginger and have two children, Jimmy and Kristi. He also completed a tour in Vietnam and night school at College of the Desert. In the mid-1980s, the elder Engle retired and ownership was purchased by Jim. Today, Jim's son, Jimmy, is part of the Imperial Sign team concentrating on sales. Continuity and stability are woven into the company's culture.

"There is a lot of security when customers give us a deposit. We begin the process immediately and are renowned for expediting a job through city approvals - getting it done on time, and right the first time," says Jim.

The company is a fully licensed state contractor adept at providing services required for presentation and communication with local governments to secure permits. Staff is experienced in creating sign programs and concepts for office and industrial complexes, shopping centers and individual businesses.

Imperial Sign specializes in design, manufacturing and installation. The company

"Since 1961, Indio-based Imperial Sign has been serving the Coachella Valley and High Desert communities."

also does service repair for lighting and signs.

Keeping up with the latest technology and training employees so that they have the proper tools to do their jobs successfully are paramount. Many of the Imperial Sign employees have been with the family-owned company as long as 15 years. And they are treated like family.

"We've been successful because of our dedicated staff. All of us live in the eastern valley and are supportive of each other," says Jim.

Although Indio's growth has provided Imperial Sign with its heaviest workload ever, Jim is adamant about maintaining the company's product, quality and people and not concerned about competition.

"I care about what we do." And that certainly has been more than enough for satisfied clients that include the Riverside National Date Festival, Mathis Brothers and Indio Fashion Mall.

Community involvement is also a hallmark of Imperial Sign. An active member of the Indio Chamber of Commerce, Jim participates on the mural committee which celebrates the City of Indio's rich history with bold, colorful murals — a perfect fit for someone who has played such a large role in the business community's history.

For more information: 760- 347-3566

I-10 Auto Mall Dealers Association

*W*hen Mike Burns, owner of Fiesta Ford Lincoln Mercury, embarked on his career in the automotive business, he was 25 years old. Indio had a population of around 7,000, and although manufacturers were concentrating on denser populated communities, Burns persevered.

Soon he was selling about 85 new and used cars a month and had 45 employees. As his business grew and a joint effort with Andreas Mozoras, owner of Unicars Honda, materialized, the concept of an auto mall was given serious consideration. Talks were initiated with the County of Riverside's director of development to see what plan might be developed that would make it affordable to purchase property so that other dealerships would have the incentive to participate.

Working closely with the county and City of Indio, Burns and Mozoras spear-headed the concept which became a reality. Unicars Honda, Fiesta Ford Lincoln Mercury were joined by I-10 Toyota and Coachella Valley Pontiac Buick GMC as well as Paradise Volkswagen, and I-10 Scion.

Although it was estimated that it would take 10 years to pay off the debt, it was done in five.

> "We recognized that Indio needed an auto mall on the I-10 and we made it happen. It wasn't an easy task but it was well worth the challenge."

Today, the I-10 Auto Mall is the #1 producer of sales tax for the City of Indio. And 38 years later, Fiesta Ford Lincoln Mercury is selling more than 300 cars a month and boasts 145 dedicated employees.

"We recognized that Indio needed an auto mall on the I-10 and we made it happen. It wasn't an easy task but it was well worth the challenge," says Andreas Mozoras, owner of Unicars Honda. The dealers have brought much to Indio in the way of products, service and community participation. Unicars Honda is among the top 10 dealerships in the state for customer satisfaction.

"Honda vehicles are safe, fuel efficient and reliable, and they are the greenest automobiles on the planet today," says Mozoras. Coachella Valley Pontiac Buick GMC has been the largest volume GMC truck dealer in the Valley since it opened in October 1999. "We offer a distinct method of selling and servicing new and used vehicles," says Ed Chavez, owner of Coachella Valley Pontiac Buick GMC. "We are committed to employees, our customers and our community."

Indeed, it is a leader in customer satisfaction and the Valley's only five-time "Mark of Excellence" award winner with GM.

Dennis Bala, general manager of I-10 Toyota, is enthusiastic about the future. "Toyota Motors has instituted a new program called Planet

Kaizen which designates the way cars will be built in the future with lower emissions and higher mileage standards. Also, Toyota Motors is practicing what it preaches by using solar to power manufacturing plants, recycled material in construction of those plants and by being as environmentally friendly as possible."

John Miller, co-owner of I-10 Scion, a division of Toyota, looks forward to an expanded product line. Scion was originally developed as an entry level automobile for the Gen X age group and has sold beyond its demographic expectation. Paradise Volkswagen, the only Volkswagen dealership in the Coachella Valley, was previously located in Cathedral City. Peter Livreri, who grew up in the desert and has owned the dealership for 10 years, applauds the move noting monthly car sales went from 20 to over 100. A hallmark of Livreri's operation is his accessibility to customers.

"The Beetle is the most recognized car in the world," says Livreri, who is also enthusiastic about the Volkswagen Touareg, named SUV of the Year by Motor Trend in 2004. "The future of Indio is explosive. With the number of new homes being built in the East Valley and the expansion of local businesses, our future looks extremely positive," says Mozoras.

Chavez agrees adding, "The growth is tremendous and the present leadership has a very positive attitude toward business which will drive success for the city." All six of the dealers are enthusiastically committed to the community. "As a business we're always looking at the bottom line; however, I feel it is equally important to give something back to the community," says Bala.

"I've always felt you need to give something back," says Burns who served for 11 years on Eisenhower Medical Center's Board of Trustees as well as on the board and executive committee of The Living Desert. Burns and his employees have quietly raised more than $140,000 for the spouses and families of fallen Marines who were based at 29 Palms. Mozoras has served six years on the Indio Chamber of Commerce Board and three years on its executive board. Coachella Valley Pontiac Buick GMC received national recognition when it developed a program called "It's Cool to Stay in School," which was implemented with all the Valley's school districts to help increase school attendance..

I-10 Auto Mall Dealers Association is a combined effort at the highest level.

For more information: Unicars Honda - 760- 345- 7555 or www.unicarshonda.com, Fiesta Ford Lincoln Mercury-760-772-8000 or www.fiestaford.com, I-10Toyota- 760-772-3300 or www.i-10toyota.com, Coachella Valley Pontiac Buick GMC- 760-772-9788 or www.i10gm.com, Paradise Volkswagen- 760-200-4000 or www.paradisevw.com, I-10 Scion - 760-772-2001 or www.i-10scion.com

> "The dealers have brought much to Indio in the way of products, service and community participation."

Indian Palms Country Club & Resort

When you have a 59-room boutique hotel with 27 holes of classic golf, and an inviting restaurant and bar - all tucked away in Indio, a city enjoying phenomenal growth, you have a winning combination.

"In a region best known for expensive world-class golf resorts we offer an uncompromising value. This makes Indian Palms a serious force among Palm Springs Valley destinations," says Mark Scheibach, general manager and director of golf operations.

It is also a resort with a rich history. As the story goes, famed aviatrix Jackie Cochran and her husband, Floyd Odlum, founder of Altas Corporation and chief executive officer of RKO Studios, were driving through the desert back in 1935 when they had a flat tire in the vicinity of what today is Indian Palms. The couple was enchanted with the area and purchased 640 acres shortly thereafter. The Ranch House they built as a guest house for their famous friends is today called the "Celebrity House" and is used for private parties, special events and corporate meetings.

Cochran, along with Helen Detweiler, the first professional golfer at Indian Palms, designed the first nine-hole course in 1947, which is now called the Indian Nine. Today the centerpiece for the resort facility is the 27-hole golf experience offering

> "In a region best known for expensive world-class golf resorts we offer an uncompromising value."

diverse play in a scenic setting enhanced by hundreds of mature trees lining the fairways.

INDIAN PALMS
Country Club & Resort

"Indian Palms' three nines – the Mountain, Indian and Royal – underwent extensive renovation over the past three years. Our goal was to increase playability, maintain and upgrade the course challenges while improving the overall maintenance of the course," says Scheibach.

Spacious hotel guest rooms overlook the golf course and boast numerous amenities. All are just steps away from La Palma Restaurant which features American cuisine for breakfast, lunch and dinner. The Lifestyle Fitness Center features Star Trac cardio equipment and a weight training area as well as Jazzercise, Pilates and yoga classes.

Meeting and banquet facilities include the Palm Terrace, a dramatic venue located atop the Clubhouse that can accommodate up to 300 guests. For more intimate events, the historic Celebrity House sets the stage with its original stone fireplace, wood-beamed ceilings and pinewood floors.

Currently Indian Palms Country Club & Resort is a community of 1,400 homes with 800 more on the drawing board. Although much has changed, the magic that attracted Presidents Eisenhower, Kennedy and Johnson, as well as renowned aviators and Hollywood legends, remains the same.

For more information: 760-775-4444 or www.indianpalms.com

Indio Chamber Of Commerce

*F*or 60 years the Indio of Chamber of Commerce has enthusiastically contributed to the civic and business development of the Indio community. The nonprofit organization is primarily membership and event funded with some monies from the City of Indio allocated for services rendered as the city's Visitors & Information Center and tourism promotion.

Sherry Johnson has been involved with the Chamber for 19 years - eight as a volunteer and chair for the Ambassador Committee and 11 in her current role as CEO. "I've been fortunate to be part of a tremendous resurgence," says Johnson. "When I was first hired as CEO we had around 450 members.

"Today our membership is 743." The Chamber affords numerous opportunities for businesses to network with other businesses as well as potential customers. In addition to providing advertising and publicity opportunities, Chamber staff assists with ribbon cuttings, grand openings and ground breakings. Other membership benefits include legislative advocacy as well as Chamber-sponsored workshops and seminars geared to stimulate business.

> "Chamber staff assists with ribbon cuttings, grand openings and ground breakings."

Indio is known as the "City of Festivals". Chamber sponsorship/partnership in internationally recognized special events attracts thousands of visitors to the community each year. The festivals are diverse in their celebrations of such things as art, cuisine and music. Among them are the Riverside County Fair & National Date Festival, the International Salsa Festival, the Chamber's Southwest Arts Festival®, the International Tamale Festival®, Coachella Music and Arts Festival, Indio Desert Circuit Horse Show (HITS)®, and the Native American Powwows.

Chamber members are invited to participate in ongoing committees focusing on marketing, image, business recruitment and retention, education, governmental affairs and public policy, special events and the historic mural project. The latter has created much interest with tourists and the media and currently seven bold, colorful murals brighten many buildings around Old Town and on Indio Boulevard, serving as a monument to the past and a vision for the future. Funding for the mural project has come from underwriting by private businesses and the sale of a limited edition series of "mural" prints, numbered and signed by the artist.

The Chamber's social events are great resources for networking and membership recruitment. Each year the Chamber holds a special Western Night, a Business Expo and Symposium, a Golf Tournament, Awards Banquet and an Installation Dinner. Not only are they fun but they are important fundraisers for the organization. As Indio celebrates its 75th anniversary, the Chamber is poised to continue its vital partnership as the community continues to grow and prosper.

For more information: 760-347-0676 or www.indiochamber.org

Indio Fashion Mall

Weintraub
Financial Services Inc.

Richard Weintraub, founder and president of Weintraub Financial Services, Inc. (WFS), has great plans for Indio. A fourth generation Los Angeleno, Weintraub has two decades of real estate experience in the Southern California, Arizona and New York City real estate markets. His company is renowned for being one of California's premier developers of high-end commercial and residential real estate properties.

The WFS management team has extensive experience in real estate investment including acquisition, land entitlement, property development and construction management, disposition, capital markets and corporate finance. The company brings a broad knowledge base to each transaction, including its ability to structure and close creative and complex transactions.

WFS is noted for transforming and revitalizing neighborhoods through their projects. Coachella Valley residents will be able to experience this firsthand as WFS has purchased the Indio Fashion Mall and some adjacent property.

"We want to create a lifestyle center for Indio and the Coachella Valley that reflects what the whole town is about," says Weintraub "We hope to embrace the culture, festivals, city history - to foster a sense of community."

> "Two decades of real estate experience in the Southern California, Arizona and New York City real estate markets."

Indeed, many believe that the Indio Fashion Mall, which opened in the mid-1970s, has long been ready for a makeover. And this will be some makeover, as WFS plans to invest $50 million in the project.

"Indio is a year-round city and not as seasonal as other desert communities. People need a place to dine, shop and be entertained. We hope to create a village which happens to have a great shopping experience, but is much more than just a mall," says Weintraub.

With the purchase of 30 acres in the immediate area around the mall and more acreage pending, plans are to create a 55-acre campus. Although many details are still on the drawing board, there will be a village street behind the mall that would encourage pedestrian traffic with wide walkways, exciting stores and charming kiosks. In addition, WFS would incorporate a mixed-use component with housing above some of the retail shops.

The architecture will be Old California Mission-style with a preponderance of water features, colorful gardens and red tile roofs. It will be executed by the Jerde Partnership, an

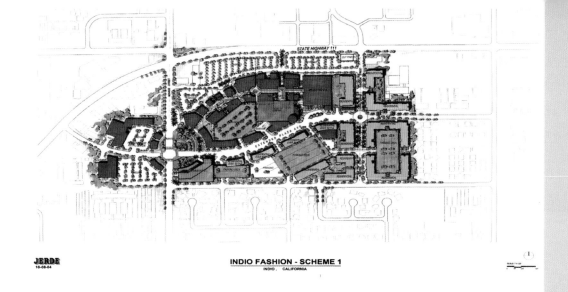

internationally acclaimed architecture and urban planning firm based in Los Angeles. The firm's philosophy is to create "experience architecture" as opposed to the traditional approach of simply putting up buildings. It is their belief that people respond to attractive and engaging architecture which provides them with memorable experiences.

The Jerde Partnership, founded by Jon Adams Jerde, FAIA, began 25 years ago when the architect was commissioned to revitalize a six-block site in downtown San Diego which is now known as Horton Plaza.

> "We want to be part of a dynamic community that stands for smart growth."

Today the portfolio includes the 1984 Olympics in Los Angeles, Bellagio and Fremont Street Experience in Las Vegas, and Mall of America in Minneapolis. And if those aren't familiar places, locally the firm is responsible for the design of The River in Rancho Mirage.

Weintraub is a fan of great architecture. His extensive travels have taken him all over the world providing him with a global concept of what ought to be brought back to Southern California. As a child, his grandmother and parents brought him to the desert, and he fondly recalls Palm Springs' famous fudge, breakfast at Louise's Pantry and an overall sense that he had come to an exotic place.

"The desert is a magical place that one must respect. Doesn't it just make sense to create a special environment here where one doesn't always need a car to have a varied experience?"

Under Weintraub's guidance, many properties have experienced the same substantial cash flow and value enhancement he plans to bring to Indio. They include:

The Venezia: one of the most recognized pieces of property in the Wilshire Corridor, this project is a ground-up construction, "Old Hollywood" style building.

The Californian: at 10804 Wilshire Boulevard, a $170 million, 23-story ultra-luxury condominium tower comprised of 85 units in 280,000 square feet of floor area. Previously, the property was under-utilized with an entitlement of merely six stories. As of November 2004, the project is 90% sold.

Saint Vibiana's Cathedral: a recently deconsecrated Catholic cathedral located in the heart of Los Angeles on the corner of 2nd and Main Street, this glorious building was erected and dedicated to Saint Vibiana in 1876. It was condemned after more than a century of ravaging earthquakes, but was rescued from demolition by the Historical Society of Los Angeles. WFS is renovating the building for public use, as well as a venue to host large-scale events. Indio comes into focus again with plans for an I-10 Freeway Power Center, a 170-acre shopping development.

"When we went into escrow, Indio had 7,000 new homes. Now there are 27,000. We are definitely here for the long term. We want to be part of this dynamic community that stands for intelligent growth."

For more information: 310-457-8960

Indio Emergency Medical Group, Inc.

Frank Curry, M.D. has a passion for solving problems. In 1983, after completing his training at Loma Linda University School of Medicine, he asked his colleagues where they thought might be the most challenging emergency room in Southern California. The answer was Indio.

Curry had a new problem to solve. When he arrived at John F. Kennedy Memorial Hospital, he discovered that residents were using the emergency room for situations that should have been handled at the primary care level.

For Curry, solutions are the answer to chaos, but there is more. "All solutions must bring positive results and be good for people," says Curry.

Today he owns the Indio Emergency Medical Group. Since its incorporation in 1994, three divisions have been introduced: West Shores Medical Clinic, the Santa Rosa del Valle Medical Clinic and the Desert Urgent Care Medical Group.

Indio Emergency Medical Group serves the emergency medical needs of the east Coachella Valley and eastern Riverside County at its J.F.K. Express Care facility. West Shores Medical Clinic serves the primary health care needs of the medically underserved community of Salton City, while the Santa Rosa del Valle Medical Group does the same

Desert URGENT Care

A Division of the Indio Emergency Medical Group, Inc.

for the communities of Coachella, Thermal, Mecca and Oasis. Desert Urgent Care is a Workers' Compensation/Urgent Care site in Palm Desert.

Curry was instrumental in creating the non-profit Santa Rosa del Valle Foundation which purchased mobile health care units that go directly to migrant farm labor camps. Next, the foundation will open the Oasis Community Clinic, an independent, free-standing facility.

Board certified in Emergency Medicine and a Fellow of the American College of Emergency Medicine, Curry is Vice Chairman of the Board of the J.F.K. Memorial Hospital, chief of the Department of Emergency Medicine and chief of J.F.K. Express Care. He also serves as chairman of the Medical Quality Review at J.F.K. Memorial Hospital, and is a member of the Child Abuse and Neglect Task Force, Riverside County.

He has been appointed a gaming commissioner for Fantasy Springs Casino with the responsibility of working with the tribe and casino management on surveillance and compliance.

As chairman of the Indio Chamber of Commerce Board of Directors, Curry looks forward to the city developing an economic plan that projects 20 years or more into the future and responsibly addresses and supports the necessary tax base and infrastructure that the city's phenomenal growth will demand. Once again, Curry is looking for positive solutions.

For more information: 760-775-4181

> "Indio Emergency Medical Group serves the emergency medical needs of the east Coachella Valley."

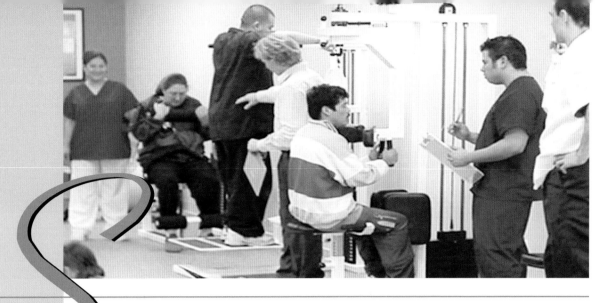

Injury Relief Care Center

Senate Bill 899 is a new legislative reform package signed into law by the Governor of California in April 2004. It is designed to provide savings by tackling mounting problems with the state's workers' compensation system. The bill went into effect on January 1, 2005.

As with any change, employers, insurers and physicians are attempting to comprehend and be in compliance with the new legislation.

Catherine Foss and Louise Bacher recognized an opportunity and partnered in creating the Injury Relief Care Center, a state-of-the-art medical facility dedicated to the treatment of auto, personal and work-related injuries. The 4,000-square-foot facility, complete with a fully equipped exercise room, opened in December 2004.

Part of the state law was the authorization of the creation of Medical Provider Networks, a group of health care professionals, joined together via written agreements with employers and/or insurers to provide medical care to injured workers as defined by the American College of Occupational Environmental Medicine (ACOEM) guidelines.

Injury Relief Care Center is one of 50 facilities in California certified and compliant with the current rulings. It is the only such facility in the Coachella Valley.

Foss, who brings 18 years of worker comp-related experience to the company, emphasizes that the goal is to see that patients get the proper treatment and that they return to work as quickly as possible.

Injury Relief CARE CENTER

Staff members include medical professionals in the field of orthopedics, chiropractics, neurology, psychology, pain management as well as physical trainers - all with established medical practices in the Coachella Valley and the Inland Empire. Administrative staff schedules appointments and handles billing and insurance paperwork for insurance companies and employers.

"It is mandatory for our administrative staff to attend monthly seminars to gain knowledge of compliancy, customer care and standard operating procedures," says Bacher.

The personal touch is also a benchmark of the new facility. "As a family-style facility we pride ourselves on personalized care, always putting patients first and making them feel at home while on their road to recovery," says Bacher.

Dr. Barry Sherwood, D.C. is delighted with the environment at Injury Relief Care Center. "It's terrific to have this qualified management staff that allows me to concentrate on providing patients with immediate rehabilitation that will give them some sort of increased mobility that very same day."

To Foss, establishing the Center in Indio was an easy decision. "There is a large workforce in Indio and we wanted to make it convenient for them."

For more information: 760-342-5151 or www.injuryreliefcenter.com

> "Injury Relief Care Center is one of 50 facilities in California certified and compliant with the current rulings."

e deliver Indio's future every day. John F. Kennedy Memorial Hospital's slogan neatly mirrors the City of Indio's extraordinary growth. Quite aptly put, since the 145-bed community hospital delivers 3100 babies a year, treats 36,000 patients in its Emergency Room, and performs 5300 surgeries annually. For years, John F. Kennedy Memorial Hospital (JFK) has been known as the "baby hospital" of the Valley - that has changed due to the population boom in the East Valley.

According to John Ferrelli, JFK's chief executive officer, "We're challenged to keep pace with the needs of an expanding population. JFK's proactive strategic planning helps to keep ahead of that curve."

Wallace Wheeler, M.D., who has practiced medicine in Indio since 1953, recalls the early years: "We had about 8,000 people in Indio then, but times have changed and we are no longer a little town. For my patients, JFK is their community hospital." The hospital opened in 1966 as Indio Community Hospital and was owned by physicians. The name was changed in 1984 to John F. Kennedy Memorial Hospital. Eunice Kennedy Shriver, the late president's sister, attended the dedication ceremony. Today, the

John F. Kennedy
Memorial Hospital
Tenet California

hospital is owned by Tenet Healthcare Corporation and is fully accredited by the Joint Commission on Accreditation of Healthcare Organizations.

With growth come advances in care. In 2004, the hospital completed a $400,000 expansion of its Obstetrical Unit, resulting in private labor and delivery rooms and additional beds for new mothers. The OB expansion was a needed addition because of the continual population increase in the East Valley and the unexpected closure of a local hospital's obstetrical unit in late 2003. Caring for children is a specialty of JFK's, as it's the Valley's only hospital with a dedicated Pediatric Unit and a dedicated education and treatment program for children with asthma. JFK is exploring the addition of a Neonatal Intensive Care Unit for high-risk babies who are currently transferred out of the East Valley for treatment. "We want to keep our patients at JFK," states Ferrelli.

Addressing the medical needs of the working population and seniors is of high priority for the hospital. JFK opened its Arthritis Institute three years ago due to the prevalence of Valley residents suffering from arthritic conditions. The Institute provides a range of orthopedic services using a team

> "We're challenged to keep pace with the needs of an expanding population."

approach. "The Institute accesses other specialized physicians, when needed, to provide advanced orthopedic services to our patients right here in the Valley," states Jonathan Braslow, M.D., medical director of JFK's Arthritis Institute. The medical staff at the hospital includes several highly trained orthopedic surgeons who provide care for Valley residents.

Physician expansion continues at JFK. Recently welcomed were two additional urologists who specialize in surgical treatments for erectile dysfunction and incontinence. The cardio-vascular catheterization laboratory (cath lab) at JFK provides full-interventional cardiology services in emergency situations. Studies show higher survival rates in facilities offering full-interventional cardiology services than in hospitals without interventional services at all. If open-heart surgery is needed, JFK works with cardiac surgeons at other hospitals for that level of care.

Interventional radiologists use the cath lab for minimally invasive procedures (MIP) as a surgical alternative. Some of these procedures include: Angioplasty stenting. Stents are small flexible tubes used to hold clogged blood vessels open after angioplasty or to open bile ducts or other pathways in the body that have been narrowed or blocked by tumors or other obstructions.

Treatments for peripheral vascular disease: Uterine Fibroid Embolization (UFE) this procedure preserves the uterus by blocking the blood supply to the fibroids, causing them to shrink. It's less cumbersome than a hysterectomy, and the recovery time is significantly reduced.

"We owe a great deal to the doctors who practice at JFK," says Ferrelli. "We appreciate

their contributions to the community. Many of our nurses are long-term employees, and they have worked with the physicians for years taking care of thousands of patients. We work as a team and it's reflected in our positive employee and patient satisfaction surveys. The bottom line is our patients receive great care and the service is second to none. I'm very proud to be a part of the JFK family."

They are the founders of the Institute for Urologic Excellence and are located on the hospital's campus. They have performed more surgical procedures addressing these conditions that any other physician in the world, and have trained many physicians on their surgical techniques to ensure quality outcomes.

Whether you've visited the emergency room, or attended a community lecture, event, or screening, you'll find that outreach and community involvement is a mainstay of the hospital's grass roots efforts to directly impact the health of the community. Indio is growing and its community hospital is growing with it to provide the medical care that will keep our community healthy and strong.

For more information: 800-343-4JFK (4535) or www.jfkmemorialhosp.com

La Piñata Restaurante

Marcos Lopez was 19 years old when he hopped in his 1941 black Chevy and headed to Indio. Lopez had grown up in the farm country of Imperial Valley and wanted to do something other than farming. Lopez liked what he saw in Indio and the Coachella Valley. True, it was also a farm community, but it was the mix of agriculture and tourism that intrigued him.

"I liked the town. It was vibrant and full of life so I decided to stay a few months," says Lopez. Fifty years later Lopez still enjoys the community, and he has played an important role in its colorful history.

When Lopez first arrived, he began applying his trade as a barber. Then he purchased Jesse Walker's Newsstand on Miles Avenue. In 1967 he went into the food business and began a chain of five restaurants in Indio and Coachella called Taco Mark.

That endeavor was the bellwether of what would become an institution in Indio - La Piñata Restaurante. Thirty-two years later the eatery on the corner of Highway 111 and Las Palmas is going strong and its reputation for great Mexican food is legendary. Today Lopez's wife, Maria, and son Damian manage the restaurant which has become a popular venue for parties, weddings and anniversaries with rooms that

> "We're challenged to keep pace with the needs of an expanding population."

can accommodate up to 100 guests.

Lopez, who enjoys the homespun wisdom of Will Rogers, might well have come across this famous quote as he was venturing into different fields: You've got to go out on a limb sometimes because that's where the fruit is.

With a fascination for real estate, Lopez began acquiring property. He bought commercial properties, 10 acres of land in the heart of Bermuda Dunes and the land for La Piñata. This proved to be his real avocation and one he continues to enjoy in a very low-key way often working as a consultant in putting together land deals for others.

His favorite Will Rogers' saying is: They're not making anymore land. Quite apropos when he reflects on how Indio has prospered over the last few years. "You must know when to push progress. Indio's time is now and the City has a tremendous future. The influx of rooftops has to be matched with a strong tax base from commercial and hotel ventures."

Lopez knows something about Indio and its progress. He has spent 22 years in local politics serving as a member of the City Council and three-term mayor. "I like people and want to do some good." Although he was urged by friends to run for office, he never thought of himself as a politician but rather as a candidate for the people who happened to have a business background. Lopez believes his major contribution during this period was the battle to keep the City in control of its water.

"I know what the value of water is. I came from Imperial Valley where water was sacred. You can find alternatives for oil, but there aren't any for water. There were some who wanted to take advantage of a $50 to $70 million transaction by selling the water. This was a three-year battle."

In the end, the City retained its ownership of its water, but this was also the end of Lopez's political career. "Never go into politics to benefit. Go in it to do some good. You can't make everyone happy, but you have to do the best you can. "Lopez has always fought for what he believes."

"To me success is when you accomplish all of the things you wanted to do in a lifetime. You can't do it all, but I've always done what I've

wanted to do. You don't have to know everything, but you can surround yourself with people who have the knowledge that you need to have."

This goes for La Piñata Restaurante. Lopez encourages his waitresses to keep up with the changing clientele which now is a mix of retirees and young professionals. He revels in the infusion of a changing marketplace and mentality and encourages everyone to stop thinking small.

He feels blessed to have lived in the Coachella Valley, to have a beautiful and talented wife, and to have had four wonderful children. Lopez has always been interested in youth and feels that everyone should try to do something for children. Years ago he was president of the Coachella Valley Girls Club, Inc. which later was to become the YMCA Girls, Inc. He helps raise funds for the Christian School of the Desert and is assisting Our Lady of Perpetual Help Catholic School with land acquisition for a new school.

Lopez considers his children to be his greatest accomplishment and continues to be active within his community and businesses. To paraphrase his mentor Will Rogers, Lopez never met a man he didn't like (that doesn't mean he always agreed).

For more information: 760-342-1183

> He feels blessed to have lived in the Coachella Valley, to have a beautiful and talented wife, and to have had four wonderful children. Lopez has always been interested in youth and feels that everyone should try to do something for children."

Landmark Golf Club

Landmark
Golf Club

*W*hen it comes to catching the vision of golf community development, few do it better than Ernie Vossler and Joe Walser, Jr., principals of Landmark Golf Company, who have led their team of professionals in the design, building and/or management of more than 50 golf course facilities including PGA West, Mission Hills Country Club, and La Quinta Hotel Golf & Tennis Resort.

In the late 1990s - prior to the building boom in Indio, Vossler and his team sparked the growth on the north side of I-10 in Indio by developing a new golf community - Landmark Golf Club which boasts 36 holes of championship golf, a full-service clubhouse, banquet pavilion, expansive practice/instructional areas, an adjacent residential community, and a vacation ownership village. Open to the public, the uniquely designed golf courses are punctuated with rolling dunes of wildflowers and foothills of natural desert terrain. Designed for professional golf events and to promote the spirit of the game, the Club's two courses marry the traditions of golf with the power of the land.

"Undeveloped northeast Indio was ready! The City of Indio offered an attractive combination of conditions and opportunities for development of a successful golf community. The city council and city staff wanted responsible aggressive development, and the city was cooperative to work with in accomplish-

> **"More than 50 golf course facilities including PGA West, Mission Hills Country Club, and La Quinta Hotel Golf & Tennis Resort."**

ing our mutual goals. The price of the land worked for development, and there was a definite community need for challenging championship golf for resident and resort play," says Vossler.

At its very beginnings, Landmark Golf Club captured international attention. Landmark Golf Club opened as "The Home of The Skins Game" from 1999-2002 and attracted top PGA Tour players such as Tiger Woods, Fred Couples and Phil Mickelson. Recognition also came from *Golf Digest* which rated the courses 4.5 out of a possible 5.0. The Desert Sun Reader Poll named the Club the desert's #1 golf facility, and Landmark North was rated the #1 public course by local pros in *Desert Golf Magazine*.

Owned by LB Hills Golf, LLC, Landmark Golf Club is managed by Landmark Golf Company. Other facilities managed by Landmark include Shadow Hills Golf Club in Indio; SilverRock Resort in La Quinta; The Golf Club of California in Fallbrook; The Ranch Golf Club in San Jose; and Mountain Falls Golf Club in Pahrump, Nevada.

With additional management contracts on the horizon, the Landmark vision continues.

For more information: 760-775-2000 or www.landmarkgc.com

Lennar

With a full portfolio of successful new-home communities throughout coastal California, Lennar - one of the nation's largest and most respected home-building companies - is establishing a firm presence in Indio and throughout the Coachella Valley.

This is clearly evident by Lennar's already robust offering of new-home communities in this rapidly growing area. Examples that epitomize the resort fairway lifestyle are two spectacular neighborhoods in Shadow Hills. These include the master-planned golf and lake community of Terra Lago - highlighted by the Landmark Golf and Country Club - and Paradiso, a stunning neighborhood of elegant homes. Meeting the needs of value-conscious buyers, the choices continue with a variety of other resort-oriented Lennar neighborhoods, including the spacious executive homes of Esperanza at Desert River Estates.

By offering a broad spectrum of new-home communities, Lennar is achieving its goal of providing home shoppers from all backgrounds and lifestyles with the

> **"Lennar is one of the nation's largest and most respected home-building companies."**

opportunity to own a brand - new home in some of the most desired locations in the Southland. From young couples or start-up families seeking their first home to move-up buyers and retired couples who want to achieve their lifelong dream of owning a luxurious, estate-style residence, customers are sure to find a Lennar home that fits their unique needs and lifestyle.

LENNAR.
Quality. Value. Integrity.

"Lennar is committed to offering a variety of new home communities in spectacular Indio," said Jeff Roos, regional president, Southern California homebuilding. "These latest offerings will meet the needs and preferences of a wide variety of home buyers."

Established in 1954, Lennar has built a reputation for offering quality homes and unparalleled customer care. The company has built more than 500,000 homes throughout the United States and is committed to offering a 100% Tickled, Delighted & Happy℠ Home-Buying Experience. Lennar was recently ranked #1 in *Fortune* magazine's list of America's most-admired homebuilders for the second consecutive year.

Lennar has always been dedicated to meeting the needs of its new homeowners. The company's TDH experience includes one-stop shopping with Lennar's own lending and escrow companies. Lennar also reaches out with "dusty shoe home previews" during construction, TDH parties designed to acquaint homeowners with neighbors and Lennar team members, and celebratory home orientations at escrow's closing. Finally, Lennar goes the extra mile with 30-90- and 360-day follow ups after move-in to ensure an extraordinary Tickled, Delighted and Happy℠ home buying experience.

For more information: www.lennarfamily.com

Mary Flores-Blandon

Many have heard the old adage that if we are served a few lemons in life, some of us can make lemonade. This well applies to the stunning career of Flores-Blandon who we suspect can also make a fine pitcher of lemonade.

As a young mother raising three children, Flores-Blandon spent her early years working as a waitress at Cielito Lindo and Coco's.

Along the way her keen sense of observation served her well. Flores-Blandon's father was in his early twenties when he purchased his first semi truck. Soon he was the proud owner of A. R. Martinez Trucking. Flores-Blandon recalls with pride and affection that even though her father spent many hours working, he always managed to make it home for holidays and birthdays. The impression his dedication to his family and work made on the young girl was one that would endure.

Later her food service background landed her a waitress position at La Quinta Hotel Golf Clubhouse. She stayed at the Clubhouse for a dozen years during which time she was promoted to food and beverage director. It was here that she would meet Ernie Vossler, who was senior vice president of Landmark Land Company, Inc. Vossler's team had a management meeting every weekday at 6:30 a.m.

> "In fact 80% of her business are referrals from past clients, who appreciate honesty and dependability."

"I was always trying to beat the boss to work in the morning as early risers impressed him. Working in the hospitality industry and country club atmosphere trained me to never say 'no' to a customer. I worked seven days a week during the season and all holidays. Perfect training for selling real estate," says Flores-Blandon.

Her first exposure to realtors occurred at the Clubhouse. She thought how wonderful it was that people could get paid for looking at houses every day. "How hard could this be? All I have to do is pretend a house is a hamburger and I certainly know how to sell those."

In 1996 she began her new career in real estate. A year later she married Mario Blandon

who had worked with her at the Clubhouse.

Having grown up in the East Valley, she wanted to concentrate her sales efforts in that area at a time when the average sale price of a home was between $70,000 and $90,000.

"Most realtors were not willing to work this market; however today the majority of these properties have realized a value increase of 3.5 times or more." Flores-Blandon was involved in many of her client's first home purchase and sale. Now as she works in residential real estate she sees that what once were first-time buyers are now upgrading to newer developments in Indio and she in turn is asked to handle the sale of their primary homes. In fact, 80% of her business is referrals from past clients.

As part of Re/Max Real Estate Consultants in La Quinta, Flores-Blandon has built a strong team consisting of business partner and husband Mario Blandon, a listing/buyers agent. Her two daughters are also part of the team. Arlene is a listing/buyers agent and Geraldine is escrow/office coordinator. Flores Blandon has trained and introduced her brothers, Robert and Al Martinez, into the real estate market and her sister-in-law into the escrow division. Her son, Greg, is also involved in the industry working for a title company in customer service while he attends College of the Desert.

"In 2002 she received the first annual Business Woman of the Year award from the Coachella Valley Mexican American Chamber of Commerce."

"Our team enjoys the challenge of educating property owners and buyers how lucrative an Indio address is, not just now that the market is booming, but over the past nine years. We have a knack for treating our clients as they are our one and only. And we actually return calls, which is unheard of if you ask anyone that has ever been involved in a real estate transaction. The key is handling real estate as a business. We have the person who answers the phone. We have the listings and buyers agents. We have a team that has become expert in these past nine years.

Her hard work has not gone unrecognized. In 2002 she received the first annual Business Woman of the Year award from the Coachella Valley Mexican American Chamber of Commerce. Her team has been the top-selling team at Re/Max in La Quinta and among the top 50 teams for all Re/Max agencies in California and Hawaii. From 1999-2002 her sales earned her membership in the agency's Platinum Club and she was inducted into the "Hall of Fame" in 2001. In 2003 she was named to the Chairman Club.

In 2004 her team was responsible for more than $25 million in sales. And one more accomplishment. She and her husband welcomed their first son, Tristen, into the world on December 3, 2003.

For more information: 760-779-4635 or www.maryfloresandco.com

Outdoor Resort Motorcoach Country Club

According to Randall Henderson, director of resort development for Outdoor Resorts Motorcoach Country Club, Indio is hands down the motorcoach resort capital of the United States. He should know. Henderson, who founded Outdoor Resorts of America in 1969, has developed 25 resorts and currently has 15 outdoor resort properties nationwide with more under development.

The company's philosophy is to add an additional scope of accommodations to existing resort communities. Its properties totally negate the dated perception of trailer parks.

Outdoor Resorts Motorcoach Country Club on Avenue 48 in Indio offers 400 landscaped sites with concrete pads of which 136 are along a scenic waterfront that boasts private boat docks around a mile-long navigable waterway. With many of the motorcoaches priced at more than $1 million, owners expect a level of amenities found in any prestigious community.

There is a 7,500-square-foot clubhouse with restaurant, bar, pro shop and a fully equipped fitness center. An executive nine-hole golf course with golf cart paths, three lighted tennis courts and three swimming pools all with spas, bathhouses and laundry facilities are also part of the luxury amenity package.

> "There is a 7,500-square-foot clubhouse with restaurant, bar, pro shop and a fully equipped fitness center."

Standard lots are 40 by 115 to 125 feet. Pull - in sites can be chosen along the golf course or along the waterways which are approved for up to 18-foot electric boats with up to 7-1/2 horsepower motors. There are also wall lots which allow for private backyards.

Outdoor Resorts Motorcoach Country Club is the third property Henderson has been involved in in the Coachella Valley. Motorcoach Resort & Spa is directly across the street, and the company's first property, located on Ramon Road in Cathedral City, at the time was the largest single tourist accommodation in the state of California.

Henderson reflects on his desert experience as being most positive. "I was fortunate when we came to the Coachella Valley to meet Pat Murphy and Frank Bogert (former mayors of Cathedral City and Palm Springs, respectively) who had a wealth of knowledge about the area. I looked at marketplace studies and had a lot of confidence in the Valley. And I liked that Indio was willing to listen to the idea of building a motorcoach-only resort."

Henderson also points out that residents of the Outdoor Resorts Motorcoach Club are affluent with 100% discretionary time and income to be spent at local restaurants, shops and grocery stores.

"Every day is Saturday."

For more information: 760-863-0789 or www.motorcoachcountryclub.com

Swank Development Company

SDC

William E. Swank Sr. has always been an entrepreneur. A licensed architect, he launched Swank Architects in 1959. SDC (Swank Development Company) is a successor to that company which he founded and now operates with his son, William Swank Jr.

Managed by a highly skilled team of professionals and associates, SDC specializes in the development of hotels and has a long history of successful hospitality ventures throughout Asia and the Mideast as well as in Southern California. And it does it all from design, build, own, market and operate its hotels and resorts. Although duties are loosely split, the son focuses on the marketing and management while the father is involved in the design, planning and construction.

SDC has been quietly headquartered in La Quinta for the past 14 years. The reason most Coachella Valley residents have never heard of SDC is because the company has built its business through its international hotel reputation rather than publicity. "We believe in letting the quality and success of our projects speak for us," said Swank.

"The Coachella Valley has a lot of vitality. We have lived all over the world but live here by choice," says Swank. "It is clean, safe and we feel a part of the community." During the 1960s and 1970s the company developed Hilton and Holiday Inn products in Southern California. Then Swank concentrated on building five-star hotels in major international markets such as Bahrain, Qatar, Singapore and China.

For the last 20 years SDC has been engaged exclusively in the development of Marriott brand hotels. As a qualified Marriott developer, SDC buys franchises and then designs, builds and operates each one as a separate entity. In the spring of 2005, SDC will open a Marriott Springhill Suites in Boise, Idaho. Like the Coachella Valley, the Swanks see great potential in the Idaho market and are looking at two additional hotels in this area.

Locally, the company built the Marriott Courtyard & Residence Inn in Palm Desert. Currently there are two hospitality projects on the board - one in Indio and one in Palm Springs. SDC's sister company, Western Pacific Resort Development, is building a large timeshare resort at the Landmark Golf Club in Indio. The first phase of the resort, which will be located on 27.3 acres bordered by the golf course, is slated for completion this year.

The company has high praise for the City of Indio. "The City and elected officials work together to support the current renaissance Indio is enjoying. Council, city management and planning are consistent and respectful of our time and money, a real pleasure to do business with," Swank noted.

For more information: 760-777-1557

> "We believe in letting the quality and success of our projects speak for us."

Rilington Communities

RILINGTON COMMUNITIES

*A*lthough Mickie and Hansi Riley and four of their six children are new residents of the Coachella Valley, they have already made a significant impact.

Their family-owned business, Rilington Communities, focuses on acquiring property, designing, building and selling homes. Among the local projects under at some stage of development are: Bella Canto, Prado and Pasa Fino in Coachella; Affresco, Ballare, Palazzo, Savannah and Avante in North Indio, Shadow Hills; Dolce in Palm Desert; and Collage in Desert Hot Springs.

Prior to moving to the Coachella Valley in December of 2004, the Rileys resided in San Diego. Since the early 1970s Mickie has been involved in all aspects of construction and development.

In 1989, Hansi and Mickie started The Riley Company concentrating on contract and fee building for developers as well as rehab and custom homes. In 1996 the Rileys saw the market turning and felt the time was right to start a development company that would be a springboard for training their six children in the business. They named their company Rilington Communities.

"We had a goal of creating a business environment for our family and company that was fun and dedicated to the excellence in our

> **"Rilington Communities, focuses on acquiring property, designing, building and selling homes."**

communities. We have a passion for what we do and build, and a genuine appreciation for the desires of our homeowners. It is more like a lifestyle than a corporation. Hansi and I personally oversee every aspect of design, including landscaping and architectural. We believe we bring that personal touch, and design homes and communities as if we were moving in ourselves."

Without a doubt the Rileys have achieved their goal. All six of their children are involved in Rilington Communities either full- or part-time. Kathleen is director of sales; Erin is director of marketing, and Kenny is involved in project support. Leslie works part-time in decorating; John in Web services, and Richard does field work. While Mickie runs the company as president and CEO, Hansi is vice president and oversees marketing and all design and creative functions.

Rilington Communities has built thousands of homes - from entry level to multimillion dollar - throughout Southern California. They have completed neighborhoods

in Fallbrook, Temecula and San Marcos, and are currently developing communities in San Diego, Imperial and San Jacinto. After experiencing increasing land costs, spiraling fees and unnecessary delays that came with doing business in the San Diego marketplace, they researched a dozen or more markets in California and decided to move to the Coachella Valley. The family was enthusiastic about the quality of life that could be had here and recognized that the market was on fire and as such would be a great place to grow their business.

"The refreshing business environment of the Coachella Valley is huge. Nationally the market has slowed. Even parts of California have slowed; however, the Coachella Valley has moved forward. This is one of the most exciting, diverse markets in the country." So delighted are the Rileys with the Coachella Valley that they are in the process of relocating their headquarters to an 8,100-square-foot building they have purchased here. More than 90% of the San Diego staff and their families will be calling this area home.

"To see the growth of the people in Rilington is as equal for us as seeing the growth in the company. The effect our success has had on many is often overwhelming and always appreciated. True success and joy is accomplished only when giving and sharing. In fact, we have implemented programs to help our staff purchase homes in the Valley."

The company has tripled in size and has acquired a dozen new projects in the building and planning stages. With revenues in excess of $125 million and a staff that now numbers 55,

Rilington Communities has never lost sight of its strong beliefs based on family values, honesty and commitment to high quality in design, features and construction of its homes and communities.

"There is nothing more fulfilling than to drive through our communities 10 years later and see children playing, grandparents walking, and an overall mature, safe environment for people to live. Hansi and I want to be part of the communities we can be proud of for many years and beyond our lifetimes. It is a small way for us to make a difference."

The Rilington staff enjoys working with the City of Indio and considers the City a member of its team intent on striving to improve the entire environment. It views growth as benefiting business, government and the community.

"We are delighted to be here and I thank the entire Coachella Valley for embracing my family and our company with open arms. It is not only our desire but our obligation to give back to the community that has and continues to be so good to us."

For more information: www.rilington.com

Waste Management Of The Desert

Although Waste Management, Inc. is the leading provider of comprehensive waste and environmental services in North America, the company tailors its services to meet the needs of each customer group and to ensure consistent, superior service at the local level.

Waste Management of the Desert is committed to developing strong community partnerships while preserving the environment. It is among the proud sponsors of numerous Indio events including the International Tamale Festival, the Southwest Arts Festival and Family Fun Fest.

In addition, it has partnered with the Desert Sands Unified School District in creating an Earth Savers Program designed to inspire and energize students into becoming better "enviro-citizens."

In the City of Indio, Waste Management provides free commercial recycling to all businesses. The company works with the city to make recycling a household habit for its residents. With the institution of "co-mingling," recyclable items such as paper, glass, aluminum, plastics, cardboard and tin containers can now be placed together in a designated gray recycling cart. Maroon containers are provided for regular household trash while green containers are dedicated to all organic materials generated from yard work.

> **"In the City of Indio, Waste Management provides free commercial recycling to all businesses."**

And it all works. California cities have been mandated with the passage of AB939 to divert a minimum of 50% of their waste from landfills. The City of Indio in partnership with Waste Management has achieved a 58% diversion rate for the last reported year. This exceeds the state average of 48%.

Customer service is at the very core of operations. Bulky Item Service for large items that won't fit into regular trash carts can be made with one call to Waste Management. Televisions and computer monitors can be picked up at no charge or taken to the Waste Management site in Palm Desert. Holiday foliage and used motor oil are recycled at no charge. "We have an operator answer our phones," says Frank Orlett, Waste Management division president. "In fact, it is part of our customer service program that our operators are required to pick up the telephone in a designated number of seconds so that no one has to wait to have their questions answered or problems resolved."

Orlett, who has been with the company since 1991, serves on the Executive Board of the Coachella Valley Economic Partnership and is actively involved in youth sports throughout the Valley. At Waste Management of the Desert, it is all about community partnership.

For more information: 760-340-2113 or www.wmdesert.com

Western Pacific Resort Development

When it comes to timeshare and resort development in the western part of the United States, few do it better than Western Pacific Resort Development (WPRD). The company is a six-year-old partnership between Swank Development Company (SDC) and the Quiring Corporation.

SDC, headquartered in La Quinta, has an impressive history of designing, building, owning, marketing and operating hotels and resorts in Southern California. Its history dates back to 1959, when it was founded by William E. Swank Sr.,

a licensed architect. Today the elder Swank shares responsibilities with his son, William Jr.

The Quiring Corporation, located in Fresno California, has been in business for half a century and has played an important role in the management and construction of some of California's most recognizable structures. The combined expertise of the design and construction professionals of these two successful organizations has been melded into WPRD, a design/build construction company fully capable of handling multimillion dollar construction projects on time and within budget.

Locally, WPRD is building a $56-million luxury vacation ownership resort in the rapidly growing Shadow Hills area on 27.3 acres bordered by the

> "The combined expertise of the design and construction professionals of these two successful organizations has been melded into WPRD."

Landmark Golf Club in Indio. The family-friendly, Mediterranean-style resort will consist of 454 condominiums that will include studio, one-, two-, and three-bedroom floor plans, as well as penthouse suites. Each condominium will have a complete kitchen, spacious living areas, air conditioning, washer/dryer, gas fireplace, TV, DVD player, compact disc stereo system, complimentary Internet connection and furnished private veranda.

Amenities will include three manmade lakes, two swimming pools, two children's wading pools, one "lazy river" pool, five courtyard spas and a children's interactive pool. There will also be tennis and sport courts, an exercise room, multipurpose game room, lounge, media room, boutique and business center.

The first phase of the luxury vacation ownership resort is scheduled to open in the summer of 2005. It has been projected that the development's first phase alone will generate nearly $13 million in payroll and an average of 310 construction jobs. In addition, the resort will provide 200 full-time equivalent hospitality jobs and generate an estimated $1.5 million in room tax each year.

"We are delighted to be in Indio. It is a great community with a terrific business environment. We enjoy working with the City's professional staff and we are exceptionally pleased to have the opportunity to develop one of the Valley's finest destination resorts," says William E. Swank Sr.

For more information: 760-777-1557

Profiles of Excellence

ABC Recovery Center, Inc.
44-374 Palm Street
Indio, CA 92201
760-342-6616
www.abcrecovery.com

The Ames Group
81-711 Highway 111, Top Floor
Indio, CA 92201-5489
760-345-2555

Best Western Date Tree Hotel
81-909 Indio Boulevard
Indio, CA 92201
760-347-3421
www.datetree.com

**Boys & Girls Club of
Coachella Valley**
83-100 Date Avenue
Indio, CA 92201
760-836-1160
www.bgcofcv.org

City of Indio
100 Civic Center Mall
Indio, CA 92201
760-342-6500
www.indio.org

Clark's Travel Center
82-253 Indio Boulevard
Indio, CA 92201
760-342-4776
www.clarkstravelcenter.com

Coachella Valley Printing Group
45-140 Towne Street
Indio, CA 92201
760-347-7316
info@cvprinting.com

**Coachella Valley Pontiac
Buick GMC
I-10 Auto Mall**
78-960 Varner Road
Indio, CA 92203
760-772-9788
www.i10gm.com

**The Design Collections and
Upholstery Outlet**
82-871 Miles Avenue
Indio, CA 92201
760-342-7887
bcpsca@aol.com

Eaton & Kirk Advertising
47-159 Youngs Lane
Indio, CA 92201
760-775-3626
www.EatonKirk.com

Events by Joe Scarna, Inc.
82-850 Miles Avenue
Indio, CA 92201
760-347-8881
www.eventsbyjoescarna.com

Fantasy Springs Resort Casino
84-245 Indio Springs Parkway
Indio, CA 92203
800-827-2946
www.fantasyspingsresort.com

**Fiesta Ford Lincoln Mercury
I-10 Auto Mall**
78-990 Varner Road
Indio, CA 92203
760-772-8000
www.fiestaford.com

**Granite Construction
Company, Inc.**
38-000 Monroe Street
Indio, CA 92203
760-775-7500
www.graniteconstruction.com

Guy Evans, Inc.
82-585 Showcase Parkway
Indio, CA 92203
760-343-1299
www.guyevans.com

Horse Shows in The Sun
319 Main Street
Saugerties, NY 12477
845-246-8833
www.HitShows.com

**I-10 Scion
I-10 Auto Mall**
78-650 Varner Road
Indio, CA 92203
760-772-2001
www.i-10scion.com

**I-10 Toyota
I-10 Auto Mall**
78-980 Varner Road
Indio, CA 92203
760-772-3300
www.i-10toyota.com

Imperial Sign Co. Inc.
46-120 Calhoun Street
Indio, CA 92201
760-347-3566
impsign1@aol.com

**Indian Palms
Country Club & Resort**
48-630 Monroe Street
Indio, CA 92201
760-775-4444
www.indianpalms.com

Indio Chamber of Commerce
82-921 Indio Boulevard
Indio, CA 92201
760-347-0676
www.indiochamber.org

**Indio Emergency Medical
Group, Inc.**
81-893 Dr. Carreon Boulevard, Suite 4
Indio, CA 92201
760-775-4181
facurry@ienginc.com

Indio Fashion Mall
82-227 Highway 111, Suite A-2
Indio, CA 92201
760-347-8323

Injury Relief Care Center
45-080 Golf Center Parkway, Bldg. B
Indio, CA 92201
760-342-5151
www.injuryreliefcarecenter.com

**John F. Kennedy Memorial
Hospital**
47-111 Monroe Street
Indio, CA 92201
760-775-2619
www.jfkmemorialhosp.com

La-Piñata Restaurant
81-921 Highway 111
Indio, CA 92201
760-342-1183

Landmark Golf Club
74-947 Highway 111, Suite 200
Indian Wells, CA 92210
760-775-2000
www.landmarkgc.com

Lennar
5000 Calle San Raphael, Suite C-5
Palm Springs, CA 92264
760-325-4289
www.lennarfamily.com

**Mary Flores-Blandon
RE/Max Real Estate Consultants**
78-411 Highway 111
La Quinta, CA 92253
760-779-4635
www.maryfloresandco.com

**Outdoor Resorts Motorcoach
Country Club**
80-501 Avenue 48
Indio, CA 92201
760-863-0789
www.motorcoachcountryclub.com

**Paradise Volkswagen
I-10 Auto Mall**
79-050 Varner Road
Indio, CA 92203
760-200-4000
www.paradisevw.com

Rilington Communities
30-885 Date Palm Drive
Cathedral City, CA 92234
www.rilington.com

**Swank Development
Company**
78-060 Calle Estado
La Quinta, CA 92253
760-777-1557
weswanksr@aol.com

**Unicars Honda
I-10 Auto Mall**
78-970 Varner Road
Indio, CA 92203
760-345-7555
www.unicarshonda.com

**Waste Management of
the Desert**
41-575 Electric Street
Palm Desert, CA 92260
760-340-2113
www.wmdesert.com

Weintraub Services, Inc.
P.O. Box 6528
Malibu, CA 90265
310-457-8130

**Western Pacific Resort
Development**
78-060 Calle Estado
La Quinta, CA 92253
760-777-1557
weswanksr@aol.com